Interpersonal Skills

Professional Development Series

Author:

Dr. Marlene Caroselli
Center for Professional Development
Rochester, NY

SOUTH-WESTERN
———————— ™
THOMSON LEARNING

Australia • Canada • Mexico • Singapore • Spain • United Kingdom • United States

SOUTH-WESTERN

THOMSON LEARNING

Vice President/Executive Publisher:
Dave Shaut

Team Leader:
Karen Schmohe

Project Manager:
Dr. Inell Bolls

Production Editor:
Carol Spencer

Production Manager:
Tricia Boies

Executive Marketing Manager:
Carol Volz

Marketing Manager:
Chris McNamee

Marketing Coordinator:
Cira Brown

Manufacturing Manager:
Charlene Taylor

Art and Design Coordinator:
Stacy Jenkins Shirley

Cover and Internal Design:
Grannan Graphic Design, Ltd.

Compositor:
Electro-Publishing

Printer:
R.R. Donnelley/Crawfordsville

Rights and Permissions Manager:
Linda Ellis

Gain the Insight to Professional Success

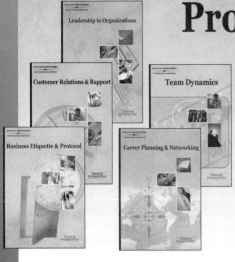

Keeping pace with today's competitive marketplace is a challenge.

Although technology has enabled us to communicate and produce in ways we never thought possible, there are other essential elements to achieving professional success. *The Professional Development Series* is a quick and practical resource for learning non-technical strategies and tactics.

0-538-72463-3	Business Etiquette & Protocol
0-538-72527-3	Customer Relations & Rapport
0-538-72484-6	Leadership in Organizations
0-538-72474-9	Career Planning & Networking
0-538-72485-4	Team Dynamics

The 10-Hour Series

This series enables you to become proficient in a variety of technical skills in only a short amount of time through ten quick and easy lessons.

0-538-69458-0	E-mail in 10 Hours
0-538-68928-5	Composing at the Computer
0-538-69849-7	Electronic Business Presentations

Quick Skills Series

Quickly sharpen the interpersonal skills you need for job success and professional development with the Quick Skills Series. This series features career-related scenarios for relevant and real application of skills.

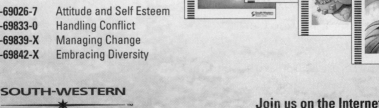

0-538-69026-7	Attitude and Self Esteem
0-538-69833-0	Handling Conflict
0-538-69839-X	Managing Change
0-538-69842-X	Embracing Diversity

SOUTH-WESTERN
™
THOMSON LEARNING

Join us on the Internet
www.swep.com

Contents

Preface

It has been estimated that 95 percent of our workplace success depends on an understanding of other people. That figure is echoed in the words of Don Petersen, former head of Ford Motor Company, who maintains that "results depend on relationships." By studying this module, you are taking an important step toward increasing your workplace productivity and improving your workplace relationships— whether you are dealing with people one-on-one or in a group setting.

Message to the User

Interpersonal Skills is organized into nine topics for easy reference. The topics provide an overview of the key elements needed to succeed in the workplace today. The module is designed to serve as a reference guide as you progress through your career. The following is a brief overview of each topic:

1. People Skills Do you have what it takes to build alliances, to establish harmony, to create an "esprit" for your "corps"? This module will help you answer these questions in the affirmative as you learn more about the human element — yourself in the process. You will discover the role of listening, feedback, and paralanguage in successful communications. You will also view assertion as a positive and necessary tool in harmonious relationships.

2. Persuading The key to leadership today, according to expert Ken Blanchard, is influence, not authority. This topic will show you how to extend your influence by using a number of influence tools. You will be surprised at how easy they are to understand and how quickly you can begin to employ them. Finally, you will see how persuasion can make problem solving more collaborative and make people feel more motivated.

3. Thinking on Your Feet Lee Iacocca once asserted that the best thing you can do for your career is to learn to think on your feet. You will gain an understanding of what the master communicators do to keep their wits about them when challenged or when asked an unanticipated question. Once you know the techniques, you can use them in personal and professional situations. You can also use them to bring out the best in others.

4. Leading Others To lead is to effect positive change. You will acquire numerous tools for helping others accept the changes that life and organizations thrust upon them. You will also acquire techniques for gaining approval for the changes you are proposing.

5. Empowering Others Power does not flow to invisible people. This topic will show you how to gain greater visibility and greater power so you can create new and improved organizational realities. You will learn why effective leaders are comfortable with power and how you can exert/maximize your power to achieve effective and ethical results.

6. Coaching and Mentoring Others If you are interested in developing interpersonal skills in order to advance your organization's mission, you will find a wide array of ideas for doing so in this module. You will learn the differences between coaching and mentoring and when to use each to help others grow and to help the organization benefit.

7. Acquiring Political Savvy The naive believe they can accomplish things on merit alone. The astute know it takes more than merit to get things done—it takes political savvy. You will learn in this topic how to enhance your political skills without sacrificing your personal standards.

8. Teambuilding Ninety-five percent of U.S. business organizations employ teamwork. Unfortunately, many of them are doing so in a haphazard fashion. You will learn, among other things, the three secrets that guarantee team meetings will get results. You will also learn about motivation, task and maintenance behaviors, and techniques that bring "esprit" to the "corps."

9. Handling Conflict This topic will examine several techniques to use when conflict rears its frightening head. Then you will have an opportunity to apply these techniques to real-world situations. You will learn what to do and what not to do in critical circumstances.

Features

Each topic begins with a list of goals entitled "At the Core." The goals are followed by an in-depth discussion of key concepts. Each topic ends with a recap of key ideas presented. Each topic also includes several quotes to serve as reinforcement and to challenge you to think about the topic in review. Online resources for further research are provided for every topic. Case studies for critical thinking are also included at the end of this module.

About the Author

Marlene Caroselli, Ed.D., a graduate of the University of Rochester, is an international keynote speaker and corporate trainer for Fortune 100 companies, government agencies, educational institutions, and professional organizations. She has conducted training in over half the states in the United States. She has also presented abroad in Guam, Singapore, Montreal, and Brazil. She has further served as an adjunct professor at UCLA, Clemson University, Michigan State University, and National University. She has served as a manager for Trizec Properties, Inc., and has held training contracts with the Department of Defense and with such Fortune 100 firms as Lockheed Martin, Northrop Grumman, and Allied-Signal. Her corporate clients include Eastman Kodak, Xerox, Bausch & Lomb, Mobil, Chevron, Rockwell, Hughes Aircraft, and Magnavox. Numbered among the federal agencies with which she has worked are the Departments of Labor, Transportation, Agriculture, and Interior; the General Services Administration; and the Bureau of Indian Affairs.

In 1984, she founded the Center for Professional Development and began adding books to her list of professional achievements. Her first book, *The Language of Leadership*, was chosen as a main selection by Newbridge's Executive Development book club. Since that publication, she has written 45 additional books.

A recent book, *Principled Persuasion: Influence with Integrity, Sell with Standards*, was named a Director's Choice by Doubleday Book Club. Her latest book, *One-to-One for Managers*, has been selected by Barnes & Noble for an online course.

Dr. Caroselli also writes frequently for Stephen Covey's *Executive Excellence*, for the International Customer Service Association *Journal*, and for the *National Business Employment Weekly*, as well as for numerous other print and electronic publications.

Further, she makes presentations for organizations such as The Executive Committee, the Mortgage Bankers Association, the Institute for International Research, The American Society for Training and Development, the Public Relations Society of America, and Professional Secretaries International.

Pre-Assessment Activity

Directions: Read each of the following statements carefully. Circle T if the statement is true and F if the statement is false.

1. T F Psychology is but a small part of good workplace relationships.

2. T F Listening well means listening to both what is said and what is not said.

3. T F You should ask the person with whom you are talking if he or she wants your feedback.

4. T F List reduction refers to minimizing the causes of a given effect.

5. T F The best problem solvers are more creative than analytical.

6. T F You can use questions as an ethical guide to your behavior.

7. T F Leadership and the ability to communicate well are closely related.

8. T F The ability to think well on your feet can be acquired.

9. T F Quotations can be used for both skill-building and practice and also as tools in real-life situations.

10. T F Leadership means effecting positive change.

11. T F You should avoid attempting to acquire power.

12. T F Leaders build alliances.

13. T F Empowerment is a one-way street.

14. T F The Five IN model refers to better communication.

15. T F Coaching and mentoring are two completely different roles.

16. T F If you have a mentor, you should also be a mentee.

17. T F Only poorly managed workplaces engage in politics.

18. T F Being political can help your career.

19. T F You should suggest a trial period if you think your proposal will not be accepted.

20. T F The team purpose should parallel the organizational mission.

21. T F Conflict in newly formed teams is an expected stage of development.

22. T F Team members will have few questions at the first meeting.

23. T F There are detectable signs of potentially violent behavior.

24. T F Saying "Calm down" is an effective means of reducing tension.

25. T F As an effective leader, you can handle every kind of conflict yourself.

1
People Skills

AT THE CORE
This topic examines:

➤ **THE HUMAN ELEMENT**

➤ **LISTENING**

➤ **FEEDBACK**

➤ **PARALANGUAGE**

➤ **ASSERTION**

I t stands to reason that if you lack people skills, you lack the ability to get things done. No matter how brilliant your mind, how extensive your computer skills, how organized your files, if you are not relating well to coworkers, you are simply not optimizing your efforts. What is worse, you are not optimizing *their* efforts either. With over 90 percent of U.S. organizations engaged in teamwork, you must be able to work well with others and utilize good interpersonal skills if you wish to optimize your work.

You no doubt already possess good interpersonal skills, but you are probably an advocate of "continuous improvement," wanting to get even better than you already are. You will have a chance to do that as you learn more about human psychology, listening, feedback, and paralanguage. You will also have a chance to test your assertion skills and to pick up some new techniques for putting them to good use. If you are ready to begin the race for which there is no finish line—in other words, your self-improvement journey—then let's get started.

> *"To laugh often and much; to win the respect of intelligent people and the affection of children; to earn the appreciation of honest critics and endure the betrayal of false friends; to appreciate beauty, to find the best in others; to leave the world a bit better, whether by a healthy child, a garden patch, or a redeemed social condition; to know even one life has breathed easier because you have lived. This is to have succeeded."*
> — **Ralph Waldo Emerson**

The Human Element

Thanks to several powerful forces at work in society and in the business world, the old hierarchy that looked to the top for leadership is crumbling. In its place, is a recognition that leadership can emerge at any level of the organization. This new perspective presents exciting opportunities for those who have a contribution to make and who can rally others to join their cause. But you have to understand others, anticipate their fears, know what motivates them, and develop working relationships with them if you are to effect positive change.

Consider these relationship-strengthening possibilities. As you read, decide which of the suggestions you are already doing, which you need to do more of, which you want to try, and which you would like to invite others to join you in doing.

- Make a concerted effort to know what is happening in the lives of those on your team. Do not be obvious, do not be excessive, and do not prod or pry or push. Do make a sincere effort to learn about each coworker.
- Once a month ask for five minutes at the start of your staff meeting to pass out a list of issues/concerns/fears/potential problems you have noticed. Invite input from the team, and have the team leader serve as moderator.
- Engage small groups in formal or informal process-improvement projects. Create a flowchart depicting the current steps in the process, then a second flowchart showing the steps of an ideal process. Where gaps occur, tackle the problem.

- Deal with a brewing interpersonal conflict or issue that is starting to divide the group—whether or not you are involved in it. These mini-eruptions in the smooth surface of office relations will ultimately create dissension if not attended to. You can serve as the hero of your own office by mediating, troubleshooting, or ombudsmanizing before the difficulties negatively impact morale.
- Few things make a work group more cohesive than pitching in to support a worthy cause. Here are a few ideas for you to explore.[1]

Award Your Own Eponyms. There are the Tonys for theater, the Emmys for daytime television, and the Oscars for movies. Name an award for someone in your workplace who is truly exemplary in terms of a particular organizational value. (Do not limit yourself to current employees.) Who *really* serves customers? Who *really* knows how to lead a team? Who *really* emphasizes quality? That is the person whose first name you should use as the award recognizing the particular qualities he or she demonstrates so well. Once the award has been established (and a ceremony held to recognize the individual), subsequent recipients can be regularly identified and given the award with considerable fanfare.

Start Your Own Kwanzaa. Dr. Maulana Karenga initiated the observance of ancient African virtues the same year Dr. Martin Luther King, Jr., was assassinated. More than 30 years later, 28 million people worldwide spend seven days in December affirming unity, self-determination, collective work, cooperative economics, purpose, creativity, and faith. Gather colleagues to specify certain workplace (or other place) values. Determine how those values can be recognized. Give the ritual a name, pick a time for its observance, and begin spreading the word.

Follow the Footsteps of Retirees. Let your retirees be remembered far beyond their retirement parties. Ask each for an old shoe before he or she officially leaves. "Plant" the shoe in a small plot of land near the entrance to your building. (Consider naming it "The Retirees' Walk of Fame" or some other title that honors those who came before and whose shoes employees can aspire to fill.) Put potting soil in the shoe, and plant a few seeds. Post a small laminated sign showing the name of each retiree and the dates of employment. Then let the fame flowers begin to grow.

> *"Questions focus our thinking. Ask empowering questions like: "What is good about this? What is not perfect about it yet? What am I [we] going to do next time? How can I [we] do this and have fun doing it?"*
>
> **—Charles Connolly**

Ideally, the question you are asking yourself right now is "What action can I take to bring about better office relationships?" Several choices have been provided here. Which will you put into action? How will you measure the effectiveness of your choice?

Listening

Apart from the long-term project you might be undertaking, you can develop your interpersonal skills by developing your listening skills. One way to determine your development is to assess yourself periodically. To how many of these questions can you answer yes?

1. Do you watch facial expressions of others as you talk with them?
2. Does your expression show sincere interest?
3. Do you maintain eye contact throughout exchanges?
4. Do you give feedback to show you are interested? How?
5. Do you deliberately avoid interrupting others while they speak?
6. Do you maintain a comfortable distance from others?
7. Do you paraphrase to check your understanding?
8. Do you inquire about the feeling behind the words?
9. Do you work at not finishing sentences for other people?
10. Do you show respect for the opinions of others who disagree with your viewpoint?

To verify the accuracy of your self-assessment, ask others to assess you on these same criteria. The wider the discrepancies between your opinion and theirs, the more work you have to do. It will help to keep a log. Recording progress is an excellent way to develop the self-awareness that precedes true change.

> *"A person without a sense of humor is like a wagon without springs—jolted by every pebble in the road."*
> **—Henry Ward Beecher**

When you listen well, you are in effect telling the other person that he or she is worth listening to. Such an exchange goes a long way toward cementing mutually respectful workplace interactions. There is another benefit too. By listening well, you can often find the exact word you need for a response. Often these words lend humor to the situation. To illustrate, when Liz Carpenter served as press secretary in the Lyndon Johnson White House, she managed to write a book, despite her heavy schedule. The book was generally well received, and one day the historian Arthur Schlesinger approached her with a backhanded compliment: "I read your book, Liz," he informed her. "Who wrote it for you?"

If you were listening well, the word *read* may have triggered the word *wrote* in your head since *reading* and *writing* naturally go together. If so, you may have been thinking of a comeback like the one Ms. Carpenter gave: "I'm so glad you liked it, Arthur," she replied. "Who read it to you?"

Of course, the use of sarcasm is not recommended. It destroys rather than builds good interpersonal relationships. At times, however, it may be appropriate to respond in kind, as Liz Carpenter did.

Listening well includes listening to both what is said and what is not said. When you are attuned to the emotion behind the actual words, then you are listening empathically. You can test the validity of your assumptions about the speaker's underlying feelings with a gentle probe, such as "You feel very strongly about this, don't you?"

Just as it is important to "read between the lines," it is equally important to "listen between the lines."

Feedback

There are people who ask for feedback, making them easy to deal with. Of course, there are also those who would rather not hear what you have to say about their behavior. With the second type, you have to tread carefully. These recommendations will help.

- *Be ready.* Plan what you will say in advance. Decide which statements will serve as the best guides for the person seeking self-improvement. Then consider the impact each of these statements will have. Find the words that allow you to say what must be said in the kindest way possible. Anticipate likely reactions and be ready to respond to them.
- *Be a builder, not a destroyer.* Self-confidence is a surprisingly fragile asset. It can be torn, sometimes irreparably, by a single thoughtless statement. When you must give negative feedback, do so in a way that builds, not destroys.
- *Be specific.* Neither vague praise nor vague criticism is of much benefit. Your comments should be pointed, but not painfully so.
- *Be committed.* Plan on follow-ups that will ensure that action plans are put into action and not put on a shelf. Set up a regular schedule of monitoring meetings.

> *"There are two ways of spreading light: to be the candle or the mirror that reflects it."*
>
> **—Edith Wharton**

When you are giving feedback, you are, in a sense, spreading light. At certain points, you are the metaphoric candle, lighting the way into the darkness of unknown behavioral territory. At other times, you are reflecting back to the individual both the positive and negative elements of his or her behavior. These tips should help you validate the person's strong points and lessen the discomfort that accompanies feedback about weaknesses.

- Ask the person receiving the feedback if and when he or she would like to discuss your observations. If the person is not receptive, your suggestions will lose at least half their power to effect improvement.
- Include both facts and anecdotes/illustrations to make your points.
- Do not make too many points at once. Do not drown the receiver with too much data. Give him or her a chance to "come up for air."

©PhotoDisc, Inc.

- Avoid game playing. While open-ended questions are good, they should not be used at the beginning of the exchange. Asking the receiver "How do *you* think you did?" is a form of entrapment.
- Work hard to keep the exchange two-sided. On occasion, pause and allow the other person to share his or her thoughts on what you just said.
- Do not waste time, energy, or emotions on issues the other person cannot change or over which he or she has no control.
- From time to time, remind yourself that the only reason for giving feedback is to help the other person become better than he or she already is. Candor is valuable, but your role is to provide more than a candid assessment. Your role is to effect improvement.
- Ask for feedback about your feedback.

> *"Kings stand more in need of the company of the intelligent than the intelligent do of the society of kings."*
> **—Saadi, Gulistan poet, 1184-1291**

While it would not be wise to assume that *all* kings (and others of their ilk) need intelligent responses, you may assume that many people in positions of power appreciate receiving intelligent feedback. In the next section, you will learn how paralanguage can make your message stronger. In the final section, you will learn how assertiveness can lend intelligence to those messages.

Paralanguage

Paralanguage refers to those elements that convey the words you have chosen for your message. Loudness versus softness, a rapid rate versus a slow rate, a highly inflected tonal quality versus a monotone—all of these elements make a difference in how your message is received and perceived.

Assess yourself on your use of paralanguage elements. Then ask a few people whose opinions you respect to answer these same questions about you. Compare your answers to theirs.

1. Do I use pauses effectively?
2. Do people ever tell me I talk too fast?
3. Do others regularly ask me to talk more loudly? Less loudly?
4. Does my voice convey confidence (as opposed to nervousness) when I have to make an important presentation?
5. Is my voice interesting to listen to?
6. Do I ever alter my natural pitch to make a point more emphatic?
7. Do I enunciate clearly?
8. Have I ever tape-recorded my voice for several minutes to learn how I really sound to others?
9. Can I project my voice to the farthest corner of a room without screaming?
10. Does my body language parallel the points I am making?

Ideally the answers were all "yes" except for Nos. 2 and 3. If not, discuss improvement possibilities with those who use paralanguage well. Then make an action plan and record your progress.

Assertion

How would you respond in this situation? Assume you have been invited for dinner at the home of a prominent politician. You are in the middle of saying grace when the politician shouts, "Speak up! I can't hear a thing you're saying!" Would you:

(a) Say, "Oh, I'm sorry."
(b) Speak more loudly as you finished the prayer.
(c) Say (politely but firmly), "I wasn't addressing you, sir."

The last answer is the one Bill Moyer actually gave Lyndon Johnson when he served as press secretary to the President. Note he did not apologize or acquiesce, but he did assert.

To assert yourself is to take what is rightfully yours—in the most gracious manner possible. Those who assert themselves have better health than those who serve as metaphoric doormats for others to step on. And the good health benefits start as early as preschool, as this headline states: "Bossier preschool kids are healthier."[2] The article begins as follows: "Assertive preschool children show signs of much better health than the classmates they boss around."

This is not meant to be an endorsement of bossy or bullying behavior. However, according to researchers at Berkeley, children who speak up for themselves rather than remain in subordinate positions have lower levels of stress and subsequently better health than children who allow others to control them.

Further reinforcement of this research comes from Yale University, where research revealed that people who were able to exert some control in their lives diminished the risk of heart attack. Nonassertive secretaries who work for demanding supervisors, according to an article in *Executive S.O.S,*[3] may be six times more likely to have heart disease than their managers.

What can you do to assert yourself and become healthier in the process? Begin by speaking up in relatively unimportant circumstances, working your way up to more significant situations. Commit to making one assertive display a week, and keep a log of your progress. You might start, for example, by firmly but politely telling someone who moves ahead of you in line that you have been waiting longer. "Excuse me, but I believe I'm next" usually works quite well, sometimes eliciting an apology from the person who may not have been aware of the transgression.

Once you gain the confidence that comes from knowing you do have some control over your destiny, you will find yourself speaking up at staff meetings or performance appraisals or when inappropriate remarks are made about you or others.

RECAP OF KEY CONCEPTS

- Make a concerted effort to know what is happening in the lives of those on your team.
- Engage small groups in formal or informal process-improvement projects.
- Deal with a brewing interpersonal conflict or issue that is starting to divide the group.
- You can improve your listening skills by assessing yourself periodically and asking others if your assessments are accurate.
- Train yourself to heighten your sensitivity to both the content of the message and the emotions that surround it.
- When offering feedback, spend some time in advance preparing for the situation.
- Keep the ultimate aim of feedback constantly in mind: you are working to build a better set of skills in the person with whom you are speaking.
- Keep your comments specific, and make the feedback process an ongoing one.
- If the paralanguage couching your words is inappropriate, you can speak slower (or faster), louder (or softer), with pauses (or without), with inflection (or with a deliberate, emphatic monotone).
- Being more assertive is a result of being willing to practice your assertion skills. Start in small ways and move on to become a habitual asserter.

2
Persuading Others

AT THE CORE
This topic examines:

➤ **COLLABORATIVE PROBLEM SOLVING**
➤ **COLLABORATION STEPS**
➤ **PROBLEM-SOLVING TOOLS**
➤ **MOTIVATION**
➤ **INTEGRITY**
➤ **TRUST**
➤ **VISION**

I t is easy to influence. It is much harder to influence with integrity. Whether you persuade for a living or simply "sell" your ideas in the normal course of learning, living, and working, you have already discovered persuasion techniques that work. In this module, you will learn to apply those techniques in different ways and you will pick up some new techniques as well. You will be encouraged to persuade for positive reasons and to influence others with your ethical examples.

> *"As human beings, our greatness lies not so much in being able to remake the world...as in being able to remake ourselves."*
> **—Mahatma Gandhi**

Collaborative Problem Solving

As an ethical persuader, you are working to improve a small corner of the world. You believe that small corners can be re-made, just as processes can be re-engineered, missions can be revisited, and attitudes can be readjusted. This belief enables you to perform your best as well as bring out the best in others.

Ideally, you should know more about your thinking style so you can optimize it based on the types of problems you will encounter. Problem solving, to be sure, depends on both creative and analytical skills. Because different problems require different solutions, the best problem-solvers have trained themselves to be lateral in their thinking; that is, they use the scientific approach when a problem calls for it or they use a more divergent style when required. Are you able to apply both types of thinking equally well? Consider the following checklist:

There are no right or wrong answers. The checklist is designed only to indicate your problem-solving inclinations. Circle *Yes* or *No* to indicate if a statement is like or unlike your typical behavior.

1. When directions are given to me, I tend to write them down (as opposed to visualizing what has to be done).   Yes   No
2. I prefer to read instruction manuals (rather than experiment on my own).   Yes   No
3. When I'm trying to remember someone, I visualize a name more easily than a face.   Yes   No
4. I pride myself on being organized, good with numbers, and detail-oriented.   Yes   No
5. I prefer to work with and within a small corner of the big picture.   Yes   No
6. I have difficulty generating multiple solutions to a problem in a short period of time.   Yes   No

Interpretation: If you had three Yes answers and three No answers, then you probably do use both types of thinking skills equally well. A majority of Yes replies suggests a dependency on your analytical skills, whereas a majority of No answers implies a more creative bent.

Why is it important to know what your problem-solving style is as well as the style of those with whom you will be collaborating? If you are not careful, you just might surround yourself with people who think exactly as you. This lack of diversity, according to research from Yale and other institutions, may impede your progress. A mix of creative and analytical team members will show more productive results than a team composed of all creative or all analytical types.

> *"Everybody can be great because anybody can serve."*
> **—Martin Luther King, Jr.**

Collaboration Steps

Influencing with integrity, not surprisingly, means exerting positive leadership, effecting positive change. In fact, author Ken Blanchard observes that the key to successful leadership today is influence, not authority. If you wish to lead others, you can no longer depend exclusively on the power of your position. (Even if you do not have an official position of leadership, you can, as the Reverend Martin Luther King, Jr., reminds us, serve your organization by leading others to implement improvements.)

However your authority, such as it is, carries less weight today than it did in times past. Because the quality movement emphasizes empowered behavior and because flattened organizations spell leadership opportunities for everyone, you cannot rely exclusively on the trappings of power. You must rely on your ability to persuade others to the worth of your cause.

Realize that the initial reaction to many of your leadership proposals may be a healthy skepticism. Most people are slow to change. They have adopted an "if-it-ain't-broke-don't-fix-it" attitude. Thus, to be effective, you must withstand and overcome the reluctance that is the usual response to a leader's initial suggestion. You and your ideas must be strong enough to withstand a range of negative reactions— from apathy to complete refusal.

Influencing with integrity may mean overcoming objections, igniting passions, or changing minds. It may involve convincing through information, persuading through personality, or swaying through strategic alliances. No matter what means or combination of means you use, the purpose behind your efforts must be an ethical one—to effect positive change for you and others.

©Digital Stock

If your efforts are less than admirable, others will eventually learn of the unethical stance you have taken. Not only do you stand to harm your reputation, but you may harm your career as well. Every action you take has consequences—either positive or negative. Sometimes you do not learn of the ripple effect you have created until long after you have spoken or acted. Whenever you set out to influence, you are tossing words onto smooth surfaces of paper, computer screens, or minds. For this reason, integrity should guide your attempts to influence. In addition, the more tools you have at your disposal, the more effective your influence can be. Those who are limited to the metaphoric hammer, view every influence situation as a nail. The more effective influencers, though, have acquired several different integrity tools and several different influence techniques.

These are some of the steps they take to build workplace harmony, especially important in situations that require problems to be solved. You, as a powerful persuader, can do what the best of them do.

1) *Create esprit de corps.* You serve as a coach when you rally your troops around a common cause. You make your vision their vision and bring about cohesion by building self-confidence. Whenever possible, make others aware of what your team is attempting to do.
2) *Ensure that goals are shared.* There are numerous ways to keep a team focused on it's task. Use visual means—post a banner in the meeting room, state the purpose at the top of the agenda, begin minutes with a mention of the goal, perhaps even have T-shirts made up stating what the team is working on. Celebrate mini-successes and keep everyone apprised of the progress being made.
3) *Recognize collective individuals.* Remembering that we do live in an age of paradox, it is not so strange to recognize individuals who are part of a problem-solving team. You want to praise the team as a whole; however, you do not want to lose sight of the unique contri-

butions different team members have made. The trick is to ensure that each person receives praise for a different reason, and the praise is given on an on-going basis. You would not, for example, read off a laundry list of accomplishments all at once. It lessens the impact of hearing the compliments. Instead, you might compliment one or two people at a meeting, send one or two team members a thank-you note, and privately thank one or two team members for their contributions.

4) *Establish a climate of challenge.* One of the most popular sayings of the quality movement was this: "If you always do what you have always done, you will always be who you already are; you will always have what you have already got." When you and your team solve a problem successfully, change will result. And change worries many people. To develop collaboration not only among team members but also among those who will be impacted by the new solution, you must to point out repeatedly the benefits to be realized from the solution.

> *"A life is not important except in the impact it has on other lives."*
>
> **—Jackie Robinson**

Problem-Solving Tools

Successful solutions are bound to have positive impacts on the lives of many people. In addition, even when the solutions fall short of their mark, the process of implementing the solution may improve interpersonal relationships within the group and show others outside the group the extent of the group's commitment to the project. These tools will help you define the problem and determine a course of action.

Brainstorm. One of the simplest tools used in collaborative problem solving is one of the oldest. More than 70 years ago, an advertising executive likened the process of collaborative idea generation to a storm occurring in the brains of the people sharing their thoughts.

In time, the process acquired a few safety precautions to use in the middle of this exciting storm:

- Reserve judgment. Do not criticize.
- Record all ideas.
- Listen carefully to all ideas.
- Try to piggyback on what has been said.
- Do not discuss until all ideas have been put forth. Permit idea owners to make changes, eliminate, reword, add to their ideas, and so on.

Reduce the list. Once you are sure everyone has had an opportunity to share his or her ideas, narrow the list. Depending on the importance of the choice you are making and the amount of time you have, you may wish to use a multivoting technique. Look at all the recorded ideas. Combine where possible, eliminating duplicates and those choices that are not realistic. Then ask the group members, working individually, to write down one-third of the items they consider worthwhile to pursue. (In a list of 20 choices, for example, each person would select seven.)

Tally the votes for each item, and list that number beside the item. Cross off those that earned 0, 1, or 2 votes. Then ask the group to vote on one-third of the remaining items. Follow the same process until the list has been reduced to one or two possibilities. You can use a show of hands to determine the final choice. If you and the other team members decide both possibilities are worth pursuing, you might form two subcommittees, one for each of the final two choices.

Gather data. Some problems your group faces call for creative solutions. (Brainstorming is especially valuable at such time.) Other problems require a more scientific approach, which calls for the collection of data to determine if you really do have a problem and, if so, to what extent it is impacting the workplace. Once you have your facts in hand, you can take a more reasoned approach to finding a solution and implementing it.

Motivation

What truly motivates others? What motivates you? What makes people so excited that they are willing to make small (and sometimes large) sacrifices to create a new reality around a concept or cause?

Motivation is but one stepping stone on the slippery slope of human emotions. Motivation is a complex issue but certainly one worth thinking about.

Some of it's complexity can be attributed to the leader. What exactly do leaders do to inspire others? As a leader, are you doing these things? Here is a quick way to find out. Answer yes or no to the following self-assessment:

1. I believe in what I'm doing.
2. I'm a good enough communicator to ignite the imagination of others.
3. I can share my fascination in a way that stirs others.
4. I actively work to develop confidence in others.
5. I regard myself as only one part of the whole picture of success.

> *"I am grateful for all my problems. After each one was overcome, I became stronger and more able to meet those that were still to come. I grew in all my difficulties."*
>
> **—J. C. Penney**

Motivation and attitude are opposite sides of the same coin, as the Penney quote suggests. If you had fewer than three yes answers to the questions above but you have the attitude of a continuous learner, you can create the following conditions for those with whom you are collaborating:

- Ensure that the task before you is challenging but not daunting. In other words, you should be able to accomplish it given the resources available to you.
- Create a meeting time and place in which team members can concentrate without outside interference on the important work they have to do. Your team deserves environmental protection.
- Ensure the goals are clearly defined, and briefly renew interest in them whenever possible.

- Give feedback to the team, and obtain it from key people outside the team when you can. Do not wait until the end of a project to let the team members know how they are doing.
- Create the realization that the project team members are working on, while part of their job, is sufficiently different from their regular job duties and that its newness will allow them to escape ordinary job frustrations.
- Allocate both authority and responsibility so team members are empowered enough to see the project through to its completion.
- Make sure collaboration is truly happening. If it is, individual concerns will recede as the solution gets nearer. Then foster the feeling of collective success.

Integrity

> *"Anything you do is everything you do."*
>
> **—Buddhist proverb**

This statement is a reminder that within your every action, your every communication, your every exchange lies the potential for both positive and negative consequences. The choices are often difficult, but help is available—in the form of questions you can ask, people you can turn to, and definitions you can create.

Is *integrity*, as the dictionary implies, a question of honesty? Is it a matter of sincerity or of uprightness? Would you equate integrity with sound moral principles? If so, what exactly are those principles?

Some people regard integrity as the decision to live according to the Golden Rule. Another consideration is the degree of integrity. Would you assess your actions as ethical ones if they brought improvement to existing situations? If not, what gauge would you use? The choices for determining what integrity means overlap with many other factors. In the simplest sense though, *integrity* means living according to specified values. But, of course, simplicity can be deceptively complex. Living by specified values involves complex ramifications and interpretations. When you act with integrity, you are widening the sphere of influence; you are using power tools to achieve powerful benefits for those who "buy" your concepts or your commodities.

If you take actions exclusively for your own advantage, you are following a narrow moral code, one that places your needs above all others. You no doubt operate within the letter of the law but perhaps not within the spirit of the unwritten laws that govern our behavior as human beings. If your actions are self-serving, you are not concerned with serving others. Consequently, your ethical influence is limited.

On the other hand, when your actions benefit other people, you are operating from a higher moral code; you are living by and influencing others with generally accepted principles of correctness rather than your own interpretation of specific rules. Unlike morality (which implies a codified sense of ethics, an acknowledged system to which many people subscribe), integrity is an individual consideration. Consequently, achieving clarity on integrity is more difficult than achieving clarity on influence. However once you have made the choices that lead to clarity, you can consciously take ethical actions— actions that reflect the principles by which you wish to live. Having grasped what integrity is, you will proceed to use it in your efforts to influence others in honorable ways.

Do not think, however, that once you have managed to define *integrity*, the definition will last a lifetime. In truth, integrity is a slow-moving target. Think about it. Over the years, haven't you shifted some of your views, in keeping with Emerson's insistence that "a foolish consistency is the hobgoblin of little minds"? Some of those views probably involved the definition of what it means to act with integrity.

The events or encounters that occur even after you have finally defined integrity to your satisfaction keep the target in a state of slow flux. These occurrences may be significant enough to force you to rethink your definition. You may have determined your personal set of principles; however, when those principles are put to the test, you may find they are not steadfast after all. Or, you may find that your principles do not apply to other people. Or, that certain factors cause a given principle to recede in importance. You may even modify your definition to include certain behaviors that have gained greater significance in your life. Having been betrayed by a friend or an employer, for example, you may now decide that keeping one's word is a critical aspect of integrity.

As an ethical leader, you invite others to join you in grappling with the complexities that surround the word *integrity*. Now let's explore the connection *trust* has to the whole issue of integrity.

> *"There is no problem too big we can't run away from."*
> **—Linus (character in the Peanuts comic strip)**

Trust

Ideally, trust exists among the collaborators. Think about those you trust (usually family members and close friends) and why you trust them. Although the subject of trust is a broad one, it can be narrowed to a few key factors.

- You trust those who are honest.
- You trust those who do what they say they will do.
- You trust those who are concerned about you.
- You trust those whose values prevent them from going where they don't belong—literally and figuratively.
- You trust those who are sensitive enough not to cause pain when they can avoid doing so.

You probably can add a few examples of your own, but establishing trust is obviously a matter of being concerned for other people. This concern may require you to advise team members that the problem is one you should all avoid or that management is less than receptive to the team's proposal or that certain members are not living up to their commitment. Always couch your remarks in positive terms, making allowances for possible reasons behind certain behaviors. However, do not distort the truth in an effort to be kind.

In the current economic climate, it is easy to see why trust levels are low. Employees are often insecure about job "security." They see an erosion in the numbers of full-time employees due to work that is outsourced or given to temporary employees. Many believe the organization is no longer loyal to them. Why, they ask, should they then feel any loyalty to the organization?

Persuading others to contribute in such a climate is especially difficult because stress is greater in these circumstances. So too are these by-products of low trust levels: gossip, high turnover, higher absenteeism, low morale, and less personal productivity. However, there are some things you can do to raise interpersonal levels of trust.

- As noted earlier, you typically trust family members and friends the most. Given this, think of ways to create a work environment that allows people to function like a family or like a close circle of friends. Determine what actions these two groups engage in (celebrations, for example); then make those actions a regular part of the workplace culture.
- You typically take friends and family members at their word. You do not ask them to account for their actions. You believe they are not trying to cheat you or harm you. Ideally, you are showing similar respect to your fellow collaborators. You do not check up on them unnecessarily, you don't micromanage them, and you do not treat them like children. Rather, you subscribe to philosophy found in the following quote.

"Give direction, not directions."
—General George S. Patton

Vision

Leaders such as Patton, who have a vision of what an ultimate outcome should be, inspire a similar vision in their followers. This creation of a shared vision eliminates the need to continually check up on others. When everyone is reading from the same sheet of music, so to speak, the conductor's job is made much easier.

Vision comes from the Latin word meaning "to see." On a related note, Jonathan Swift defined *vision* as "the ability to see the invisible." When you look into the future, what do you see regarding your job, your department, your customers, and so on? If no vision of an improved (or perhaps worsened) state appears, you may want to ask some questions to help formulate a picture of a future that is better than the present.

- What is the biggest threat facing us right now?
- What will our customers demand in the future?
- How will technology impact the way we do business?
- What societal occurrences will impact the organization?
- What global issues to do we need to be concerned with?
- How are manager/subordinate relations likely to change in the years ahead?

Of course, some situations may be so apparent that you need to begin a plan of action right away. You may not have to ask questions or gather data to determine underlying forces that can erupt at some future point; questions that will lead you to take advantage of more beneficial forces may begin to poke through the existing soil of the status quo. True leaders are aware of what is happening—in the organization, in society, in the world at large—and they act upon budding problems before they bloom. Consider the words of Niccolo Machiavelli: "In the beginning, problems are easy to cure but hard to diagnose; with the passage of time, having gone unrecognized and unattended, they become easy to diagnose but hard to cure."

©PhotoDisc, Inc

RECAP OF KEY CONCEPTS

- Know the value of diversity — not only in the types of people in the group but also in the way those people think.
- Influencing with integrity means exerting positive leadership, effecting positive change.
- The key to successful leadership today is influence, not authority.
- Steps in collaboration include creating esprit de corps, ensuring that goals are shared, recognizing collective individuals, and establishing a climate of challenge.
- A collaborative problem-solving tool (brainstorming) can aid in improving interpersonal relationships.
- Motivating others means creating conditions under which they can aspire to move beyond their current circumstances.
- Integrity mean living according to specified values. When you act with integrity, you are widening the sphere of influence; you are using power tools to achieve powerful benefits for those who "buy" your concepts or your commodities.
- The safest way to establish trust in interpersonal relationships is to consider how and why trust is established with friends and family. Then work to replicate those same factors in the workplace.
- Establishing a vision is often a matter of exploring questions that lead to a specification of trends. These trends, if negative, must be reversed. If they cannot be reversed, alternatives to existing operations should be employed.

3
Thinking on Your Feet

➤ **LEADERSHIP LANGUAGE**
➤ **PREPARING THROUGH PRACTICE**
➤ **TECHNIQUES FOR QUICK THINKING**

L earning to speak well "on your feet" may be the best thing you can do for your career. At least that is the opinion of an American icon, Lee Iacocca, who maintains that the ability to express your thoughts quickly and well is critical to career success. This topic examines the importance of this skill. People are not born with quick wits; they develop them through practice and through a study of the tools used by successful speakers. That is exactly what you will be doing in this topic, gaining practice and then learning to use specific tools.

> *"Leaders who are inarticulate make us all uneasy."*
> **—James Hayes**

Leadership Language

The observation by James Hayes, former head of the American Management Association, contains an important lesson for those who depend on their interpersonal skills to get things done. If you cannot express yourself with confidence, others will lose confidence in you. If you cannot state your thoughts clearly, others will not understand the goal. If you cannot organize your ideas, others will not organize around you.

When you fumble, mumble, and stumble your way through a response—when you lose your train of thought—you are simultaneously losing your audience.

More and more, the business world expects leaders who can respond to unexpected situations with intelligence and speed. In some companies, for example, job applicants are handed a sheet of paper and told to develop a full-page ad that would convince a prospective employer to hire them.

In other companies, such as General Electric, managers must respond on the spot to suggestions made by their staff during "WorkOut" sessions. These sessions start when the manager prepares a list of problems/issues/decisions. He or she then assembles the staff and presents the list. Questions are invited, but only for clarity-seeking purposes. The manager then leaves the room so the staff can "work out" the problems. When the staff has formulated possible solutions or resolutions, the manager returns. He/she is accompanied by his or her manager and several other senior officials, who sit in the back of the room and observe while the manager responds to the staff's suggestions. The manager can either reject, accept, or postpone a decision on each of the ideas presented. Needless to say, if the manager rejects every idea, he or she may be labeled a micromanager by those observing. If the manager accepts every idea, it may seem as though the person is unable to prioritize. Finally, if the manager needs to think about every decision, he or she may appear indecisive.

If you lack the necessary verbal skills in such circumstances, you could be hampering your career. Those skills, in large measure, consist of using words correctly. We use language to communicate with one another and with ourselves. It is the basis of all our interpersonal dealings. Words serve as the bridge between internal monologues and external action. They form a cultural network of understanding. Leaders understand the power of words. You can capture this power in two ways: exercising in the nonreal gymnasium of practice situations and using language tools in the real world of workplace interactions.

©PhotoDisc, Inc.

In team meetings, for example, the leader needs to employ leadership language on a continuous basis. In many ways, you function like a coach when you lead a meeting; you demonstrate support for the winning moves of your team members. But you also cheer the team on when there is a lag in "scoring." As team leader, in both an actual and a metaphoric sense, you use words to create a cohesive team spirit. You rally your group on to victory by virtue of your ability to verbalize faith and enthusiasm. In short, you use language to lead.

Specifically, your language will reflect these elements.

- *Receptivity to the opinions of others on the team.* You must maintain impartiality as you invite ideas and opinions. On the other hand, praise is important to maintaining motivation. When you praise, do it collectively. If you do offer individual praise, make certain it's not the same individual each time who receives your praise.
- *Control over conflicts.* While you want to keep discussions moving, you also want to have several people doing the moving. To allow one person to control the discussion or to allow two disputants to sidetrack the discussion is to waste everyone's time.
- *Analysis (but not criticism) of breakdowns.* Your leadership language reveals the analysis you have done of the setbacks, pitfalls, or breakdowns in the team's efficient operation. But it should not reveal a patronizing or accusatory tone. You want to analyze as a means of moving the team forward.

Preparing Through Practice

It will not happen overnight, but you can become an outstanding thinker and speaker. You can display feats that evoke admiration in others, but becoming a mental athlete requires practice. Just as sports figures work out in a gym, you are going to work out with a series of exercises designed to develop your mind's muscles.

- *The Last-Word-Heard Reply*
  Set a timer two minutes, and ask a friend to begin speaking. When the timer goes off, your friend stops talking and you begin talking. The challenge is to use the last word your friend spoke as the first word of your two-minute talk. In addition, your talk must be relevant to the comments made by your friend. While you are speaking, he or

she should reset the timer. This exercise works best when the timer is turned away so neither of you can watch the minutes ticking away.

- *The Two-Minute Challenge*

  Work with a friend. At least once a day, each of you gives the other an unexpected challenge when you see each other in the hallway or when you meet for a break. The challenge may be something like this: "You have exactly two minutes. Give me at least seven titles that contain a color" or "List seven state capitals west of the Mississippi" or "Give me seven male/female paired names, such as Andrew/Andrea." You can make up any number of challenges for your partner. In responding to the ones made up for you, you are developing confidence in your ability to marshal your thoughts in response to a specific prompt.

- *The Question That Keeps on Asking*

  Team up with two others. You begin by asking the second person a question as the third person keeps count. The second person replies to your question with another relevant question. The "game" is over as soon as one of you makes a declarative statement or puts a tag on a declarative statement (such as "You have studied leadership, *haven't you?*"), pauses too long, or asks a question that is not relevant to the conversation. If you and your partner reach a total of ten relevant questions, you have done very well. The value of this exercise lies in forcing you to utter something other than the first thought that comes to mind. If you can train yourself to do this (and with sufficient practice, you can), you avoid the embarrassing verbal gaffes your less practiced colleagues will make.

- *The Quote Interpretation*

  Have someone supply you with a quotation you have not heard before. Then, without hesitation, give your interpretation. To illustrate, consider the meaning that lies behind these 2,000-year-old words from Virgil: "From a single crime, know the nation." Think of a crime the whole nation is/was familiar with. What does it say about the country?

- *The Strange or Substantive Question*

  You need a partner for this exercise. Prepare a list of questions. (This activity, by the way, is also excellent practice for interview situations.) Your partner does the same. Then at unexpected moments, he or she surprises you with one of the questions from his or her list—to which you must respond with no lag time at all. After a while, of course, you unexpectedly ask your partner one of your questions. This sort of practice can and should become habitual. An example of a strange question might be "Why do you think Imelda Marcos had so many shoes?" An example of a substantive question might be "If you were asked to design a new logo for our organization, what would it look like?"

©PhotoDisc, Inc.

- *The Unrelated Pair*
This challenging exercise forces you to think both quickly and creatively. Place one hundred unrelated words in an envelope. (Invite friends and colleagues to contribute words of their own.) In front of an audience of at least one other person, withdraw two words; without pausing, make an intelligent link between them. If the two words, for example, are *spider* and *trust*, and you say something such as "I see a spider crawling across the trust deed," you have given only a mediocre response. But if you say something such as the following you gave risen above the obvious, providing a creative response: "Trust has the fragility of a spider's web. It can entrap several small indiscretions as easily as a spider captures a fly. The trust web, however, cannot withstand the weight of a major betrayal, just as the real web cannot hold a thousand flies. Accumulated transgressions will destroy the gossamer threats of established trust."

- *The Forced Fit*
Here is another confidence builder. If you are successful at this exercise, you should be able to handle any situation that comes your way at work. A colleague asks you to propose an improvement plan. It may be related to environment, morale, physical fitness, meetings, and so on. You have five minutes to outline a five-step plan. The first recommendation must start with a word beginning with the letter A; the second, with the letter B; the third, with the letter C; the fourth, with the letter D; and the fifth, with the letter E.

After you have done about six or seven of these (without repeating any of the five A, B, C, D, or E steps), you are given another command: Outline a seminar session in five steps. The first step must begin with the letter H, the second, with the letter I, the third, with the letter J, the fourth, with the letter K, and the final step, with the letter L.

- *The Verboten Verb*
  This is a challenging exercise—so challenging that you must find two others to help you control your thoughts so you can think on your feet without putting them in your mouth. One of your partners chooses a verb; for example—*discuss*. This person then becomes the listening observer. You begin a conversation with the third person, who asks you an innocuous question, such as "What are your plans for the upcoming vacation?" or "What do you think about management's latest decision?" You respond to questions for about five minutes, studiously avoiding the word *discuss*. If your listening observer catches you saying something you should not say, you "lose." Your penalty may be to buy coffee for the other two during your next break. Of course, you can also keep a running tally. The first person among your triad to total ten losses is the one who pays a predetermined penalty.

> *"Speak cleverly, if you speak at all; carve every word before you let it fall."*
>
> **—Oliver Wendell Holmes**

Techniques for Quick Thinking

Now that you are in good mental condition—you have learned to control stress and have acquired confidence—you can actually use the tools for which your exercises have primed you. You will find several listed below. None will fit every situation in which you are asked to think on your feet. However, the more tools you have on your metaphoric tool belt, the more readily you can rise to the verbal occasion.

- *The P-P-F Method*
  If you are unexpectedly asked for an opinion on a topic, especially in a work-related situation, you can organize your thoughts quickly by

referring to the *Past*, the *Present*, and the *Future* in relation to the topic under consideration.

- *The F-A-S-T Approach*
  Whether you have to write a letter or give an impromptu presentation, you can sound "together" as you begin. Start by stating the *Focus*. Continue the exploration of your concept by *Amplifying* a bit on the stated focus. When you amplify, you add a little more—still in a general vein—to the purpose or initial point you made. The third step requires you to *Specify*, or give, the details related to the focus. Finally, you *Tie up* your argument or viewpoint with a concluding statement.

Here is an example. Assume your manager catches you off guard at a staff meeting by asking what you think of offering a lunchtime lecture for employees on the topic of memory development. Your response might sound like this:

"There's no doubt about it. We could all use some memory development. (Focus) As we do with other training, though, we should think about the benefits of such a course. (Amplify) For one thing, I think we could build better customer relationships if we remembered the names of our most frequent customers. (Specify) We could also improve productivity by recalling certain steps in a process instead of having to look them up each time. (Specify) And this is kind of long-term, but we could delay the onset of Alzheimer's disease by keeping our brains active now. (Specify) So in my opinion, the advantages far outweigh the cost of such a program." (Tie up)

- *The Memorized Quote*
  Commit to memory as many quotations as you can. The more you have in mind, the greater the likelihood that you can find one to use in the beginning of a response while another part of your brain is preparing what comes next.

To illustrate, recall the preceding example where your manager asks your opinion on memory development. You could begin with an appropriate quote, such as "You know, Jim, Rene Descartes once said, 'It's not enough to have a good mind. The main thing is to use it well.'" Then you could go on to list the benefits of the class: "We really have a lot of good minds around here. I think if we offered a memory class, we'd be helping our employees use their minds even better than they do now. I also think we could increase productivity and benefit in several other ways."

- *Definitions*

    When the situation lends itself to a definition, you can use one to buy some time as you gather your thoughts. For example, if you are asked during a job interview what *supervision* means to you, you might define it in terms of its Latin roots—literally, "to see" and "above." In many senses, the supervisor does oversee the work being done by others, but let's continue with the hypothetical example of your supervisor soliciting your views on the memory development class.

    Your reply, using a definition, might sound something like this: "I support those who would define memory development as learning parlor tricks to amaze their friends or recalling every song the Beatles ever sang. But for me, memory development means finding ways to make my mind work better and faster so I can get my work done better and faster."

- *Trigger Words*

    People who think well on their feet also listen well on their feet. They often hear a trigger word embedded in the other speaker's message. The trigger word helps them shape their own response almost immediately. An example of this comes from a realtor in Rochester, New York. After raising her daughter, she decided to start her own realty company and took her business plan to a loan officer at a local bank. He listened attentively and then asked, "Does your husband know you are doing this?"

    The word *husband* triggered the associated word *wife*. The realtor replied with a question of her own: "Does your wife know you are asking questions like that?" She made her point.

- *Questions*

    If you need to buy some time for yourself, consider redirecting the question asked of you back to the person who asked it. For example, if a person attacks something you have said, politely ask, "Would you be willing to share the statistics on which you have formed your opinion?" You can use many other questions to buy yourself a little more thinking time.

- *Teflon Toughness*
  Finally, you will do well to develop a thicker skin. Not all critical comments are criticisms of you. Sometimes people are simply thinking out loud about the viability of a given plan. Yes, some people enjoy making others feel uncomfortable. But if you find such a person in your midst, just remember (and perhaps even quote) the words of Dolly Parton: "I'm never offended by dumb blond jokes," she once admitted. "That's because I know I'm not dumb." She paused for a moment and then added, "I also know I'm not blond!"

> *"Speech is a mirror of the soul: as a man speaks, so is he."*
> **—Publilius Syrus**

Your speech can reflect an image of a poised, professional, and persuasive soul—even if you are caught unawares and asked to share your thoughts in front of a group. First, build your response muscles by working on the exercises suggested previously. Then flex those muscles by using the recommended tools whenever you can.

RECAP OF KEY CONCEPTS

- Leadership language is the basis of all interpersonal dealings. Words serve as the bridge between internal monologues and external action.

- Leaders work hard to acquire tools that enable them to handle the unanticipated with poise and professionalism.

- Through practice, you can become a better thinker and speaker.

- Gain experience with exercises such as The Last-Word-Heard Reply, The Two-Minute Challenge, The Question That Keeps On Asking, The Quote Interpretation, The Strategic or Substantive Question, The Unrelated Pair, The Forced Fit, and The Verboten Verb. In time, you will learn that your brain will not let you down in stressful situations.

- Those you admire for their quick-thinking wittedness were not born with the gift of seamless speech. They have worked at understanding how to formulate quick and cohesive replies.

- Techniques for quick thinking include use of the following: The P-P-F Method, The F-A-S-T Approach, The Memorized Quote, Definitions, Trigger Words, Questions, and Teflon Toughness.

4
Leading Others

"The main dangers in this life," asserted Nancy Astor, the first woman to serve in England's Parliament, "are the people who want to change everything—or nothing." The danger of extremes and the use of a moderate, middle-of-the-road approach as it relates to leading others are discussed here. Much of what you are already doing is exactly what you should be doing as an effective manager. If, as a leader, you are doing today what you were doing five years ago, you simply are not optimizing your managerial talents. The pace of change today demands a change of pace. Leadership, quite simply, means effecting positive change.

With regard to self-improvement on the leadership level, think about those you regard as true leaders. What traits to they possess? Which of these traits do you yourself possess? Think too about the actions that influence you to do your very best work. Are you replicating those actions when you interact with others?

Finally, move away from the work circle of which you are the center. Does the larger environment promote achievement? Does it inspire extraordinary efforts from ordinary people? If not, what can you do to bring about some changes?

Building Esprit de Corps

If you enjoy wearing the leadership hat, you can not act autocratically. If you do, you will not be acting long in your leadership role. (If you are not building a team, as a leader, then you are probably building loyalty or respect.) However, if you are able to unite a group of disparate individuals, trust, cohesion, and harmony will result. These ingredients are critical in the recipe for leadership success.

> *"I've got my faults, but living in the past isn't one of them. There's no future in it."*
> **— Sparky Anderson,**
> **former manager of the Detroit Tigers**

Ideally, you can help those on your team to relinquish past processes, procedures, policies, and practices that no longer function as well as they once did. You can encourage living in the present with an eye toward the future. One thing that will help is benchmarking, the process of comparing one's own operation to those considered best in the field. Through this process, benchmarkers can assess what is and is not working well in terms of their own work flow.

Within two weeks, work with your team to prepare an outline of what you would like to benchmark with an individual or an organization regarded as a leader in the field. Make the contact and follow through.

Whether or not your team project involves benchmarking, you will achieve more if you pause from time to time to analyze the present and plan for the future. Consider using the following questions:

1. What "dumb" practices exist in your work environment? (It was Sam Walton who encouraged Wal-Mart employees to "eliminate the dumb.")
2. How comfortable are you with change?
3. If it were within your power, what changes would you make to improve the present modus operandi of your workplace?

4. Do you regard yourself as a risk taker?
5. How do you use what power you have?
6. Who is or could be a champion or an advocate for your team (someone from upper management or from inside or outside the organization)?
7. How aware is senior management of your team's efforts?
8. How could your team gain even more support?
9. What prevents you from having an observer present at your team meetings?
10. What do your agendas look like?

> *"Everyone is a genius at least once a year."*
> **—Georg Christoph Lichtenberg**

Managing Others

Every leader must do some managing, and every manager must do some leading. Among the things you manage are stress, time, emotions, energy, priorities, people, attitudes, communications, knowledge, budgets, and so on. The most powerful management of all may be that of ideas and the people who offer those ideas. To ignore those thoughts or to create a climate in which they wither and die is to do irreparable harm to the organization.

> *"The greatest losses are unknown and unknowable."*
> **—W. Edwards Deming**

What are the things you can do to create a climate of creativity so those greatest losses to which Deming refers do not happen? Build and then manage the excitement that flows when people are truly energized. See if these possibilities will work in your circumstances.

- Provide some training (if only informally) on team dynamics.
- Set realistic and well-defined (but challenging) goals.
- Ensure that your team's work parallels the organization's mission.
- Post group rules.
- Monitor accomplishments.
- Turn mistakes into learning opportunities.
- Help others regard rejection as a step along the way to success.
- Celebrate successes.

Power Associated with Leading Others

> *"Above all, he gave the world, for an imperishable moment, the vision of a leader who greatly understood the terror and the hope, the diversity and the possibility of life on this planet, and who made people look beyond nation and race to the future of humanity."*
> **—Arthur Schlesinger, Jr., writing about John F. Kennedy**

Historian Schlesinger's words may not apply directly to your leadership; however his words do provide clues to the actions you must take to be an effective leader. You must understand the power you hold over others and use it to instill hope. Reverend Jesse Jackson, Jr., maintains that a leader's job is to keep hope alive. You must value diversity. You must explore possibilities. You must work to improve the future.

Position Power. The word *power* carries a negative connotation for many people. How do you view power? Are you hesitant to use it? Would you be surprised to learn that the most effective leaders are comfortable with power? They have learned to use it wisely because they know there is no other way to achieve outstanding results through collective and collaborative efforts.

You need not have position power to serve as a leader. In fact, some who hold the title of manager have not yet learned how to lead others. Related to expert power is the power derived from having information. Within any organization are those who work hard to obtain information (and sometimes gossip) and then use it to their own advantage. They dole it out to selected recipients, enjoying their role as keeper of the latest or most critical organizational news.

Expert Power. You can qualify for leadership by virtue of expert power. If you have specialized skills and knowledge that allow you to fill an organizational void, you can indeed lead others. Here are some tips for enhancing your management skills—even if you are not a manager.

- If you are an expert in some regard, you have a responsibility to let others know of your expertise. Apart from the fact that doing so increases your visibility (power does not flow to invisible people), sharing your expertise can help your colleagues.
- If you discern that a specialized kind of knowledge is needed in your office or if you would like to learn a particular skill, begin acquiring that knowledge in both formal and informal ways. You need not earn a degree in a particular field, but you can certainly acquire more information than you currently possess.
- Keep your learning goals small at first. Then incrementally increase both the breadth and depth of them. For example, if your goal is to be a better writer, you might start by gaining mastery over often-confused words, such as *effect* and *affect*. (There are over 6,000 confusing word pairs in the English language.) Once you are confident of your ability in that area, move on to other concepts, such as indefinite antecedents or the dangling participles.
- Consider creating a knowledge bank, a list of people who possess specialized work-related knowledge and a description of what that knowledge is. Circulate the list so that when others are in need, they know to whom they can turn.

Charismatic Power. If you are fortunate enough to have this kind of power, you will find others aligning themselves with you. Your charismatic personality draws others to you. This kind of power goes beyond popularity. It calls others to give willingly of their time, money, and/or effort. It is the type of power that attracts volunteers to a cause.

Association Power. If you associate with an admired individual, group, or cause, you may well acquire the power of association.

Certainly this peripheral power, is not as deep as other types of power, but it can be used for positive purposes nonetheless. If your sister, for example, is a local television anchor, you may find others wanting to be friends with you for no reason other than your association with a celebrity of sorts.

©PhotoDisc, Inc.

"Whoso would be a leader must be a bridge."

—**Scottish proverb**

Building Alliances

Whatever problem you may be having at work, someone else has also faced that problem and someone else has already solved it. All too often people believe their difficulties are unique; therefore, they hesitate to form the partnerships that can help them overcome the difficulty. Interpersonal problems are often predictable; they have a sameness about them. For this very reason, you should be reaching out to others to help you solve problems and resolve issues. You must serve as a bridge between the past and the future, the haves and the have nots, and the internal and the external.

In what ways are you currently serving as a bridge? How can you expand your bridge? What new ones can you build? Look around you. You will find many opportunities for forming new alliances. In fact, you can turn a negative into a positive, as an assistant did in a multinational company. She was mugged on her way to her car after working late one evening. She called the police that evening to report the robbery. She also called the police department the very next morning and asked if an officer could come out to address a group of assistants at lunchtime regarding personal safety. Her alliance with the police department turned into an annual lecture.

Keep the following in mind as you build your alliances :

- *Have a plan*. Haphazard overtures yield haphazard results. Your alliance partner will appreciate your having taken the time to provide a clear plan with a clear goal.
- *Reciprocate*. Whenever someone goes beyond what he or she is expected to do, find a way to respond in kind or, at the very least, call or send a note to express your appreciation.
- *Follow every lead*. If your intended alliance partner is not interested, do not give up. There are many others with whom you can form mutually beneficial alliances. When you are tempted to throw your hands up in despair, remember facts and statistics such as these:
  - Authors Jack Canfield and Mark Victor Hansen were rejected by more than 200 publishers before they found one who would publish their first *Chicken Soup for the Soul* book.
  - As a child, Einstein was told by the headmaster of his school, "Your mere presence offends me."
  - As a student at Yale, Fred Smith wrote a paper for a management professor, who deemed the concept proposed in the paper as unfeasible. That unfeasible concept became Federal Express.
  - Artist Mary Engelbreit was told by her high school counselor that her drawings were "too bohemian."
  - Decca Records executives, after hearing an audition performed by a musical quartet, gave this assessment: "We don't like their sound. Guitar groups are on their way out." The guitar group was the Beatles.
  - The MGM testing director who watched the screen test of an aspiring British actor, pronounced, "Can't act. Slightly bald. Can dance a little." Fortunately, others determined that the slightly bald, bad actor could dance a lot. Fred Astaire was his name.
- *Read voraciously*. And while reading, keep your mind open to creative possibilities. Many new ideas for alliances suggest themselves when you remain receptive to the seeds trying to sprout through the printed page.
- *Look both inside and outside for bridges you can build*. Wherever you encounter a complaint, a gripe, an office pouting, you have a chance to improve the situation by forming an alliance. Sometimes it may involve bringing together two parties who have misunder-

stood each other. Sometimes, it may mean finding an outsider who can help resolve the situation.

Planning Guidelines

We live in an age of paradox. One of the leadership paradoxes you face is the need to plan, juxtaposed with the need to acknowledge that, despite your best plans, things happen that you have no way of foreseeing. (Witness the outcome of the November 7, 2000, election.) After these events happen, of course, you can make plans to prevent them from recurring, but the tumult associated with life in these times is not something you can prevent.

> *"We cannot direct the winds, but we can set the sails."*
> **—Anonymous**

Keep in mind that some things will occur that you cannot control; there will always be organizational, economic, and national "winds" you cannot direct. However, you can and should continue to set your sails toward your ultimate goal. As you do so, keep in mind:

- Your manager's, department's, and organization's goals.
- The need to involve your teams (and others) in planning sessions.
- Events happening in the world, such as the World Trade Center bombing, and the possible impact of those events on your plans.
- Myths and assumptions that may lead you in the wrong direction as you plan.
- Your reliance on intuition as you plan. (Do not rely too heavily on intuition unless you have charted the results of decisions made at a gut level.)

RECAP OF KEY CONCEPTS

- Building esprit de corps involves helping others relinquish past processes, procedures, policies, and practices that no longer function well. You encourage living in the present with an eye toward the future.

- As a leader who manages others, you manage stress, time, emotions, energy, priorities, people, attitudes, communications, knowledge, budgets, and so on.

- Leaders should be comfortable with power. You can begin to achieve one type of power, such as expert power, then move on to charismatic power, working to develop a natural ease with others.

- Leaders build strategic alliances. In a leadership role, you must serve as a bridge between the past and the future, the haves and the havenots, and the internal and the external.

- To lead without a plan is to run the risk of wasting valuable organizational resources.

5
Empowering Yourself

AT THE CORE
This topic examines:

- ➤ **EMPOWERMENT DEFINED**
- ➤ **RESPONSIBILITY**
- ➤ **THE FIVE INS OF EMPOWERMENT**
- ➤ **EMPOWERMENT BENEFITS**

No matter who you are, what position you hold, or where you work, you probably have to report to somebody. If you are fortunate enough to work in a culture of empowerment, you are allowed control over your job (not complete control, but enough control to make you feel your opinion matters). When you are not given an opportunity to provide input, you, in time, lose interest in your job. Not only do you lose (in this case interest), but the organization loses as well. The company loses what it might have gained from your intelligence, drive, and innovative thinking.

A good illustration of the importance of empowering coworkers involves a famous golfer who warned his caddy only to speak if spoken to. In addition, he informed the caddy to answer only yes or no. Wanting nothing and no one to distract him, the golfer hit the ball through an entanglment of tree branches, above a small lake, directly onto the green. Analyzing his next shot, he forgot his orders to the caddy and asked the caddy's opinion. "What do you think, the five-iron?" The caddy replied in the negative. The golfer ignored the advice and proceeded to hit the ball inches away from the hole. In triumph, he gloated to the caddy, "What do you think of that?" He added, "You can talk now."

The caddy did not waste a moment. "That wasn't your ball, sir," he said.

Empowerment works. For proof of that, look at what others have to say about the results they attained by sharing power with all levels of the organization.

©PhotoDisc, Inc.

- American Airlines saved more than $2 million in fuel costs by letting pilots determine the fastest and least expensive ways to fly between two points. In fact, the National Aeronautics & Space Administration (NASA) estimates that the aviation industry as a whole could save well over $1 billion if such empowerment were extended to all pilots at all airlines.
- The Gallup Organization found in a recent survey that a supervisor's presence has little effect on his or her employees' productivity. In fact, 38 percent of workers polled say they are most productive when their supervisor is not around.
- Frances Hessebein, CEO of the Peter Drucker Foundation, notes, "Almost every company inherited the old hierarchy where rank equaled responsibility, and it doesn't work in today's world."
- As reported in an article entitled "Stress, Death, and the Need for Control,"[4] people who work in positions that make high psychological demands of them but who are not given much control over their work have a greater risk of heart attack (two to three times greater) than those who are empowered to make decisions regarding the work they do.

  To illustrate, an unempowered administrative assistance is more likely to develop heart disease than her manager who does not invite her opinion or ask for her input.
- The results of a University of Michigan study found links between an organization's culture and certain measurements, such as profits, market share, and return on investment (ROI). The ROI in those

organizations that actively encouraged employee participation in decision making, for example, was double that of firms with little or no employee involvement.

A question you may wish to ask yourself is "How hard am I working on empowerment?" Rate yourself on a scale of (low)1 to 5(high) to reflect the degree to which you believe the following statements:

_____ I am assertive.
_____ I ask for credit when it is due me.
_____ I propose ideas to my supervisor.
_____ I initiate projects without waiting to be asked.
_____ I am aware of organizational goals and tie them to my work.
_____ I have leadership skills.
_____ I can relate well to most people.
_____ I am willing to learn on a continuous basis.
_____ I am not easily intimidated.
_____ I would rather take action to improve a situation than complain about it.

If you are truly interested in self-improvement, you will make a copy of these ten traits and ask coworkers (and perhaps even your supervisor) to assess you. Compare their answers to your own to learn how others see you. If you discover wide discrepancies between their scores and your own, you may want to reassess your basic operating style.

Like it or not, the good old days and the good old ways are gone forever. No longer do people do what an authority figure says they should merely because he or she has authority. Employees today do not hesitate to speak up and speak out. (Witness the construction worker yelling at the President of the United States as they stood at the site of the collapsed World Trade Center, "We can't hear you!" Those workers *wanted* to hear the President and when they could not, they did not stand quietly by; they made their needs known). You can expect such outspokenness from your own employees.

If you are not yet serving in a supervisory capacity, you are nonetheless making your needs known to those who are. Those needs might revolve around the work you do and ways to improve it, but they also could revolve around other aspects of the work environment. Whenever you hear yourself or others complaining about something that should be done, you are actually hearing the voice of empowerment calling to you. Listen to it. Do what you can to effect improvement in your work environment.

Think carefully about what motivates you to do your very best work. Chances are your salary in not what is leading you to perform well. Consider the possibilities below; then select your top six motivators and prioritize them. (If you have an opportunity, also ask your supervisor to select the six he or she believes are your top motivators.)

____ Variety of tasks   ____ Knowing what I do counts

____ Acceptance by my peers   ____ Good communication policies

____ Good pay   ____ Recognition of my work

____ Lack of pressure   ____ Social outlets with coworkers

____ Steady employment   ____ Easy work

____ Good policies/administration   ____ Longer vacations

____ Interesting work   ____ Chance to participate in decisions

____ Adequate breaks   ____ Respect for me as a person

____ Incentive system   ____ Chances for promotion

____ Good working conditions   ____ Help with personal problems

____ Being "in" on things   ____ Challenging tasks

____ Precise job description   ____ Regular evaluation of my performance

____ Freedom on the job   ____ Agreement with objectives

____ Chance for self-development   ____ Attending staff meetings

____ Location of office   ____ Being given responsibility

| ___ | Having a good supervisor | ___ | Training to make me proficient |
| ___ | Many fringe benefits | ___ | Finishing what I set out to do |

___ Other (Explain)_____

Having determined your motivators and having asked others to do the same, give further thought to the items on the list. Some you have no control over whatsoever (location of office, for example). Yet, there are many motivators from which you can derive great benefit, many over which you can exert empowered control. Discuss the possibilities with others; then undertake some empowered action to effect positive change in your working conditions.[5]

Empowerment Defined

The most exciting aspect of the empowerment movement is that it gives employees the confidence to do something to alter their circumstances. Instead of being miserable on the job, empowered employees convert the same amount of work they would use to be miserable and apply it to making the situation better.

Empowerment means individuals have the freedom to make decisions that will benefit the organization and its customers. It also means, of course, that questions of authority and responsibility have been discussed and agreed to in advance.

Empowerment can be likened to a two-way street—unlike delegation, which moves in one direction (from the top down). Empowered employees can suggest improvements to their managers instead of waiting for their managers to make assignments to them. When a manager delegates, he or she is essentially asking an employee to take charge of a task and see it through to completion. The employee may not ever do that particular task again. By contrast, an empowered employee is in a permanent state of heightened authority. He or she has

©PhotoDisc, Inc.

demonstrated competence and as a result, has earned the trust of his or her manager.

The difference between empowered teams and self-directed teams is minimal. The empowered team may or may not be a natural work group. It could, for example, involve union representatives from several different divisions empowered to make certain decisions. When this empowered team has accomplished its mission, it disbands. The self-directed work team, by contrast, continues to work together by virtue of the technology, territory, physical space, and mission the members share.

Some of the questions you need to explore with your managers and colleagues are as follows:

- About what kinds of decisions do you need to consult with your supervisor?
- Over which projects do you have complete authority?
- How much empowerment do you wish to be given?
- What kind of monitoring system needs to be in place?
- Which actions require higher approval?
- How would you define the working relationship between you and your supervisor?
- What kind of reporting is required? to whom?

These and other answers will help you achieve a working definition of empowerment that best suits you, your manager, your colleagues, and your circumstances.

Responsibility

You must work harder to acquire empowerment in a distrustful, micromanaged situation than you do in a situation that gives employees freedom to work toward the organization's best interests. Before you take the additional responsibility that provides empowerment, review these aspects of your job situation. The analysis will help you determine how much responsibility to ask for. Consider the following checkpoints:

- *Management Behaviors* Where does your manager's style fall on the continuum between controlling and empowering?

- *Management Expertise* Does your manager have limited experience/training, or is his or her skill level extensive?
- *Culture* Give careful thought to the way people operate. Is the emphasis on the individual and on competition? Or is the emphasis on teamwork and cooperation?
- *Information* Do people tend to be cautious and guarded with knowledge, or are they open and sharing?
- *Interactions* Are people treated fairly, or is there the perception (and perhaps even the reality) of favoritism?
- *Diversity* Are people who are different laughed at? perhaps even mocked? Or is there evidence of both tolerance and respect for individual diversity?
- *Teamwork* Is there clarity surrounding team goals? Do people willingly join teams? Do teams get things done? Are people serving on teams requiring their particular expertise?
- *Structure* Do you have access to senior management, or are there so many layers that you can not really connect to anyone beyond your immediate supervisor?
- *Job Descriptions* Are you expected to do exactly as your job description states, or are you allowed flexibility to improve processes or suggest new ideas?
- *Partnership* Are distinctions between management and hourly workers strictly abided by, or is there the sense that collegiality and partnerships are the way to achieve goals?

> *"I merely took the energy it takes to pout and wrote some blues."*
>
> **—Duke Ellington**

It is fairly easy to complain, to whine, and to moan and groan about all the things that are wrong. And, without a doubt, there probably are some things wrong in your organization. There is no such thing as the perfect workplace, no such person as the perfect supervisor, no such reality as the perfect employee. There is always room for improvement, and the drive toward it should be continuous.

Ideally, you have the mind-set that regards problems as opportunities. You do not dwell on things that others pout about. Instead, you take that energy and assume some responsibility to make things better than they already are. The Five *In* Model that follows will assist you in determining how much responsibility you should take on for a given project.

The Five Ins of Empowerment

When you decide to assume greater responsibility than you currently have, you need to think about how much responsibility you truly want and can handle at this point in your life. The following model takes you from the lowest level of responsibility to the highest. Understand though that if your manager decides not to

©PhotoDisc, Inc.

fully empower you at this time, he or she may have very good reasons for his or her decision. If you are new to the department, for example, your manager may not yet know the extent of your capabilities. He or she would do well to limit your empowered actions until you have had a chance to demonstrate exactly what you know and can do. As your manager learns more about your capabilities, he or she will be likely to give you added responsibility.

- *IN form* At this stage, you may have done the research on a given project or topic and your responsibility ends when you *inform* the manager of your findings. He or she takes over now and sees the project through to completion. This is the lowest level of empowerment and is a good place to start if you are new to the process of assuming greater responsibility.
- *IN vestigate* When you are operating at the next level of empowerment, you *investigate*, meaning you go beyond merely acquiring data. You are moving up the ladder a notch. At this level, you make a recommendation to your manager based on what you have researched. Of course, your supervisor is free to reject your recommendation, but you have at least placed the mantle of responsibility on your own shoulders, even if you can not fully wrap it around yourself.

- *IN tend* At the next *In* level, you put your arms through the mantle's sleeves, so to speak. You have taken on a task and researched it well enough to know what you intend to do to solve the problem or move forward with the project. When you are empowered enough to operate at this level, considerable trust has been placed in you. While you still need your manager's approval to bring the project to completion, you are nonetheless very much in charge. Your manager can, of course, suggest, modify, or tell you not to proceed, but you are still tipping the scales at this stage to the point of equilibrium.

- *IN itiate* The fourth level finds you nearly in complete charge of a project. You can *initiate* both minor and major tasks without obtaining your supervisor's approval. However, you need to keep him or her informed via periodic progress reports. At this level, you are operating, if not as equals, at least as partners.

- *IN dependent* When you reach the final level, you are *independent*; that is, your manager has worked with you long enough to know the quality of your work. He or she trusts you enough to know you can handle a project from inception to completion without having to check with him or her on minor details. Upon completion of the project, you share the results with your manager, but you do not need to provide regular reports. Caution: Do not expect to begin at the Independent level unless you have already established a relationship of trust with your manager.

> *"If I had to use one word, it would be 'empowerment.' "*
> **—Robert Eaton**

Empowerment Benefits

Asked how his company was able to increase earning by 246 percent in a single year (to $3.7 billion), Chrysler's Chairman Robert Eaton pointed to empowerment. Eaton and other organizational leaders throughout the nation, even throughout the world, have found that empowered employees work more productively, more happily, more healthfully.

Studies show that improvements in quality, service, and productivity—gains of 50 percent and higher—are the result when employees are empowered to do what they believe and know is right. Part of the reason for the dramatic gains realized in empowered organizations may be explained by a 14-year study of 12,500 Swedish employees, reported in the March 1996 issue of the *American Journal of Public Health*. Researchers found that when workers were given some degree of control over their own jobs, they experienced less stress and less damage to their hearts. Less stress equates with a happier work environment, which equates with better and more work being done. Working conditions in which employees have little or no control over their own work are considered a leading risk factor of heart disease.

RECAP OF KEY CONCEPTS

- Empowerment means that individuals have the freedom to make decisions that will benefit the organization and its customers.
- Before you take on the additional responsibility that provides empowerment, review these aspects of your job situation: management behaviors, management expertise, culture, information, interactions, diversity, teamwork, structure, job descriptions and partnership.
- Consider which level of empowerment is most appropriate for you. When you INform, you merely report. When you INvestigate, you go beyond gathering facts to making a decision based on those facts. At the INtend stage, you develop a plan of action. Near the top of the empowerment scale is the INitiate level. Here you are in charge of something you have proposed but you must keep your supervisor informed of your progress. Finally, when you operate at the INdependent level, you are, for the most part, on your own.
- Studies show that when employees are empowered to do what they believe and know is right, improvements in quality, service, and productivity are the result.

6
Coaching and Mentoring Others

AT THE CORE
This topic examines:

- ➤ THE ROLE OF A COACH OR MENTOR
- ➤ TO COACH OR BE COACHED
- ➤ COACHING TECHNIQUES
- ➤ MENTORING CONSIDERATIONS
- ➤ TO MENTOR OR BE MENTORED

S everal studies have shown that organizations that offer employees personalized attention have better retention rates than those that do not. Coaching differs from mentoring in numerous ways. However, you can both coach and be coached, and you can be both a mentor and a mentee.

> *"Obstacles cannot crush me. Every obstacle yields to stern resolve. He who is fixed to a star does not change his mind."*
> **—Leonardo da Vinci**

The Role of a Coach or Mentor

Coaches usually deal with specific problems, while mentors deal with careers. Both deal with career-minded individuals determined to overcome professional obstacles. In helping those who are "fixed to stars," coaches are usually suggested or assigned within an organization while mentors are usually sought out. Typically, you work with one coach on a single problem you have. By contrast, you can and should have many mentors guiding you at the same time. (Among them might be recruiters, career counselors, and those who have achieved success in a given field.) The coach takes a narrow view of a given quality or skill, while the mentor typically looks at the big picture.

An assigned coach may be an outsider paid to provide help or an insider who may be your immediate supervisor. The mentor is working with you by choice, not by organizational mandate. Coaches may work with a team, but your mentor works with you alone. If you are using a coach, you are reacting to a specific need that has been pointed out. If you are using a mentor, you have probably made a proactive career choice.

Coaches actually provide training, whereas mentors suggest training. The coach usually has a job to do, and when the short coaching stint is complete, you may never see him or her again.
The mentor, though, will be a part of your career for a long time. Coaches are tough; they are there to point out the negative. Your time with a mentor, though, is more positive. The difference is that the coach points out things you may not have realized about yourself; the mentor tends to confirm the good image you already hold of yourself. Basically, the coach evaluates and passes judgment on snapshots of your career. By contrast, the mentor works on a film that spans a big portion of your professional life.

To Coach or Be Coached

According to an article in *Fortune* magazine, you need a coach if you are being overlooked for promotional opportunities and you do not know why.[6] If this is happening to you, you may want to consider finding someone to coach you. Know, however, that it takes a brave person to solicit feedback and, on the basis of that feedback, to take action to improve his or her style of behavior. If you have that kind of courage, you can benefit from the suggestions that follow:

- To decide if you could benefit from coaching, think about all the people you encounter in a given day—coworkers, internal customers, vendors, external customers, managers, and perhaps those whom you supervise. Take an informal survey. Ask some of these individuals what you can do to make their jobs easier, or ask what you can do to improve the relationship you already have with them. Take notes on what they say; then find someone inside or outside the organization who can coach you on providing better service or having better relationships.

- If you suspect your career problems are more serious, prepare a questionnaire that calls for honest, insightful replies. Ask coworkers to fill it out anonymously and return it to you. Be grateful for the opportunity to take action before it is too late. With the most serious charges, write out an action plan that includes obtaining advice from a well-respected management veteran.

- Set up a meeting with your manager well in advance of your performance review. Ask two questions: 1) "Here's where I am. Over here is where I want to be. How can I get there?" 2) "Will you help me meet my goal?" If the answer to the second question is a reluctant one, find someone else to guide you. That someone may be a coach or a mentor.

Of course, if you are coaching someone else, you can recommend the preceding tips to that person as well. The next section explores coaching techniques.

> *"In baseball and in business, there are three types of people. Those who make it happen, those who watch it happen, and those who wonder what happened."*
>
> **—Tommy LaSorda**

Coaching Techniques

The words of the Los Angeles Dodgers' coach have significance as they are written. However, by turning them around, you also have a good idea of the coaching process. It begins when you or a coworker wonders about a career setback. What caused this person to do what he or she did? What events led to the decision? What factors caused him or her to err? You approach or are approached by the individual to discuss a plan to overcome whatever deficit he or she has to prevent the error from happening again. You watch the improvements being put in place. In doing so, you are making career success happen.

Your coaching plan should include:

- A discussion with the coachee regarding exactly what needs to be improved.
- An assessment to learn the extent of the problem.
- A determination of steps to be taken immediately to lessen the "damage" caused by the mistake.
- An outline of steps to be taken to overcome the skill deficiency.
- A reading list so the coachee can learn from multiple sources.
- Periodic meetings to assess the extent of improvement.

The techniques you employ will vary. Just as parents, teachers, and ministers vary their approaches, so do good coaches. Sometimes they sympathize; other times they demand. They probe and prod and push. They question. They teach. They praise. They do whatever it takes to increase your self-confidence and your desire to improve.

Part of that self-confidence relates to the way the coachee expresses him- or herself. Pay careful attention if you hear statements such as these:

"I'm sorry."

"May I give you an example?"

"You've probably already heard this, but…."

"I always forget to do that."

"I've never been very good with numbers."

"I'm certain this will probably work."

Discuss ways to create a more positive, assertive tone. Instead of using the "I'm sorry" phrase, for example, the person might not say anything if the mistake was truly insignificant. If the situation warrants an expression of regret, other possibilities include:

"Excuse me."

"I didn't mean to do that."

"Please forget I just did that."

"I'm having a bad hair day." (if the occasion lends itself to levity)

Listen for other expressions (such as grammatical errors) that can damage the image of professionalism the coachee is trying to project. Help him or her overcome the bad verbal habits into which he or she has fallen.

When you meet with your coachee, bring an outline of what you want to cover in a given session. This prevents you from wasting time in idle chitchat. It also prevents you from overloading the coachee with too ambitious a game plan.

> *"We aren't where we want to be, we aren't where we ought to be, but thank goodness we aren't where we used to be."*
> **—Lou Holtz**

Make certain you end your coaching session on a positive note. Find an inspirational quotation, such as Lou Holtz's, and use it to sustain your coachee's faith in him- or herself—and in you as well.

Mentoring Considerations

Mentoring originated thousands of years ago with the *Odyssey*, Homer's wonderful tale of adventure. In that story, Odysseus' confidant and advisor, Mentor, became the teacher of Odysseus' son, Telemachus. Modern-day mentors use some of the same techniques used by the mythological figure—they guide, offer advice, share their experiences, and teach. In a survey of top executives, Heidrich and Struggles Inc., a Chicago-based executive search firm, found that 80 percent of executives had mentors at some point in their careers.[7]

Because mentoring is more career-oriented than coaching, which tends to address a single and specific problem, employees at various stages of their careers enter mentoring relationships.

New Employees. If you are a new hire, you will benefit from a mentor who can "show you the (organizational) ropes," helping you find a comfort zone in a seemingly cold and uncaring infrastructure. The unknown becomes less frightening when someone who has been there guides you through it.

Senior Employees. Even veteran employees can benefit from a mentoring relationship. Many organizations involve their senior employees in preretirement counseling, linking knowledgeable mentors with those seeking such expertise.

Women. Although women have made tremendous strides in achieving managerial success in corporate America, the gains are relatively new. As a result, many women managers, in an effort to get ahead, are eager to work with a mentor. (Unfortunately, they may not be as eager to serve as a mentor, fearing perhaps that a mentee's failure is associated with them.)

Minorities. For too many years, the upper echelons of corporate America were populated by white men. When mentoring did occur, it typically existed between an established white male and an up-and-coming white male. All of that has changed, and protégés of diverse backgrounds are now linked with mentors (not all of them white males any longer) in upper management.

Those Approaching Burn-Out. You can fulfill an important service by aiding those whose fires of enthusiasm do not burn as brightly as they once did. Your mentoring need not take the usual form. You could, for example, organize a series of lectures, inviting a number of different mentors to address, not an individual mentee, but rather a group of individuals who need their motivation embers rekindled. The group could also meet to hear from a panel of experts who have survived burnout themselves, or the group could meet to watch inspirational videos.

> "If you hear a voice within you say, 'You cannot paint,' then by all means paint, and that voice will be silenced."
> **—Vincent Van Gogh**

When you serve as a mentor, you are the voice that silences the critical (and often erroneous) voices that may be telling your mentee he or she is incapable of one thing or another. You serve as a sounding board for your mentee, listening carefully as he or she voices fear or doubt or hesitation. If you have prepared a list of "commandments," based on your own experience, you can more readily respond to what your mentor is telling you. Some of the items on your list might involve:

- *Office gossip.* Encourage your mentee to avoid it.
- *Office politics.* Encourage your mentee to use it to his or her advantage.
- *Visibility.* Paradoxically, it should be acquired in a quiet way. Making waves leads as often to a big splash as to a capsized boat. Mentees want to avoid having the latter occur.
- *Mistakes.* There is tolerance for a first-time occurrence, but criticism is justified when the same mistake is made two or more times.
- *Commitment.* While devotion to an organization is admirable, excessive devotion can lead to an imbalance of priorities and ultimately to health and family problems. Help your mentee keep things in their proper order.

> *"Basically, my job is to take a hammer and chisel and chip away the rough edges in a constructive manner."*
> **—Kenneth Reynolds, senior vice president, Stevens Graphics, Corp.**[8]

To Mentor or be Mentored

If you have rough edges, you can probably benefit from a mentor yourself. If you spot some rough edges in a new hire (even if he or she has extensive work experience), you can benefit from offering to be a mentor. Your mentee will benefit too, as will the organization, for mentored employees are more likely to remain with a company than those who do not receive such guidance.

In fact, if you have a mentor but are not mentoring someone else, you may be viewed as a person concerned with advancing his or her own career without regard for giving back to others the advantages you are receiving. Ideally, you can do both—serve as a guide to the Telemachuses in your organization and learn from the mentors who see some rough edges in you.

Whether you call it mentoring or coaching (some regard the two words synonymously; others regard coaching as a subset of mentoring; still others point to the distinctions discussed at the beginning of this module), the fact remains that you have much to offer. Many can benefit from the knowledge you have acquired over the years.

RECAP OF KEY CONCEPTS

- Coaching is short-term, specific, and generally intended to remedy a particular flaw. Mentoring typically involves a long-term relationship, generally intended to develop a career rather than a specific skill. The terms are often used interchangeably, however.
- If you have thought about some of the voids in your own professional portfolio, you could probably benefit from a coach.
- As a coach, you wonder about and then analyze what your coachee may be doing wrong. Next, the two of you work out a plan and then watch as good things happen to your coachee.
- Ideally, you will both have a mentor and be a mentor. Many are involved in mentoring relationships: those who are just entering a profession, those considering leaving a profession, those who have been discriminated against in the past, and those who are starting to feel burned out.
- You may be able to benefit from having a mentor yourself. You may also find a rough-edged colleague who could benefit from your mentorship.

7
Acquiring Political Savvy

> *"Technical ability is 90% of any job. The other half is politics."*
> **—Anonymous**

This tongue-in-cheek remark carries considerable weight as far as work relationships are concerned. Those relationships can either advance or retard your career potential. Is it possible, you may wonder, to be a political animal and still be ethical? The answer is a resounding yes. This topic explores how.

> *"Politics is the art of the possible."*
> **—Bismarck**

To some people, the word *politics* has a negative connotation. However, *politics* can also have a positive connotation. Politics can be seen as a way to make the impossible possible, the imagined real, and the scorned, proud once again. If you look at politics that way (as a means to a positive end) then you can avoid the negative connotations some people ascribe to the word.

Often the successful employment of political means is a question of good communication. Having the right words and knowing when to use them can make quite a difference when it comes to interpersonal communications. Those who have trouble finding the right words or knowing when to use them politically may quickly find themselves falling from the pinnacle of success to the flat plains of failure. Politics means not only having the right words but also knowing the right time to use them.

Criticizing the President in a national crisis or suggesting that our pilots lack courage is certainly not "politic."

If you intend to use politics to make good things happen, you must recognize the importance of influencing others with well-chosen words. Both style and substance help you convey your ideas in a politically correct fashion. *How* things are said is often as important as *what* is said. The effective office politician has a good sense of both elements. When the message you want to deliver is not encased in the proper medium, it often fails.

This checklist will help ensure that your message is politically and interpersonally correct:

- *Do you give thought to the effect your words will have before speaking or writing them?*
  Political correctness lies at the heart of effective interpersonal communication. When you are concerned about the feelings of others, you think before you speak and write, so you are expressing your ideas in a way that excites rather than incites others. The poor communicator moves ideas from his or her head onto paper and then directly to the recipient. The effective communicator reviews, reassesses, and rearranges words and thoughts for the greatest impact and the least amount of damage.
- *Do you use humor appropriately?*
  While the world appreciates a good joke, jokes made at the expense of any one group are not only thoughtless and offensive, they may also cause you serious legal trouble. You must resist comebacks that are sarcastic in tone no matter how suitable they may seem at the moment. (Always try to keep the big picture in mind. Your exchanges with a person, if they are positive, will result in better workplace harmony and productivity. If they are hurtful, just the

reverse will be true.) If you are not a naturally funny person, find a few anecdotes or humorous lines that will work in several different situations. Memorize them and use them as needed.

- *Do you seek to avoid words that will cause discomfort for others?*
Consider in advance particular words that may be offensive to others. To illustrate, to refer to a group of secretaries as "girls"; to use as verbs words that designate whole cultures ("gyp"); or to use, even innocently, a revered cultural symbol as the name of a sports team is to demonstrate insensitivity and may, quite possibly, evoke anger as well.

- *Do you use transitions to tie your ideas together?*
To show that you are paying attention to what another person is saying, make tie-ins, or connections, rather than jumping to a new topic once the other person pauses for breath. The same is true for the writing you do. Transitions help you segue smoothly and logically from one topic to another.

- *Do you employ content and context aligned with the other person's preferences?*
The tone of your communication will, of course, affect the attitude with which your listener or reader receives your message. Strive for a tone that is acceptable for the message, the audience, and the circumstances. When you have a communication that is serious in content, deliver it in a context that is equally formal and professional. For example, clip-art illustrations are not appropriate in a message that takes a firm, no-nonsense approach. On occasion, you may have to communicate in an authoritative tone. Do not dilute the strength of your content by being apologetic. Excessive humility usually fails to win over an audience. No one expects a leader who does not believe him- or herself worthy of respect and praise. Followers are willing to walk behind a leader who has achieved greater-than-average accomplishments. When a leader belittles his or her own accomplishments, followers begin to doubt the leader's sincerity or competence or both.

- *Do you think from the other person's perspective and try to understand his or her concerns?*
The egocentric leader believes the world revolves around his or her own concerns. The leader who is politically astute, on the other hand, understands the importance of seeing things from a wider

perspective. Here are questions you can ask yourself regarding your ability to wear wide-angle lenses and thus avoid myopia:

- How long have I clung to this particular view?
- Have I honestly solicited other viewpoints?
- Am I proud of my stubbornness?
- When is the last time I shifted position on an important issue?
- Do I listen to others or merely show polite attention?
- Am I threatened by those who do not agree with my viewpoint?
- Am I typically motivated by what is best for the organization or by what is best for my career?
- How important is it to me to receive credit for what I have done?
- How good am I at playing the political game?

Inevitability of Politics

Politics is an inevitable part of every organization in the United States. Politics has always been a part of the workplace and always will be. The trick is to learn to play the political game to your own advantage *and* to the advantage of others without causing harm to anyone else. Being political means getting along with others in order to move them toward accomplishing a specific goal. It does not mean maneuvering for selfish purposes, manipulating in order to deceive, or scheming so others lose while you win.

You may think you would rather avoid organizational or office politics altogether. The truth remains, however, that to make a difference, to assume leadership, or to use influence positively, you need politics in order to be effective. You can not escape office politics. It is universal but not necessarily evil. You can use it to your own and others' good.

> *"Uppermost is not being seduced by the politics of one group over another."*
>
> **—Bill Knaus**

If you do not use politics carefully, it can spell your downfall. You must think carefully and comprehensively about politics in order to maintain a neutral position. It is not enough to merely declare yourself apolitical. Being unaware of what factions exist in your office may cause you to choose sides without realizing you are doing so. However, just seeming partial to one side or the other is not the only danger.

There are other dangers too. First is the danger of being so politically naive that you miss opportunities that lie right in front of your eyes. You cannot bury your head in the sand—such actions leave your backside exposed. You need to sit up and take notice of what is going on around you. You must gain political experience so you leave your comfort zone and realize the stakes involved in the game of politics. If you are uncomfortable being a "player," you may be running away from, rather than toward, chances to move ahead and accomplish important things.

Today's employees are sophisticated. They have seen and heard the best and so are cautious about dealing with the worst. They are fully aware of the games being played—for both positive and negative reasons. If you wish to coalesce coworkers and achieve improvements in your work processes, you must communicate honestly and simply. *Trust* and *inspiration* are words that should characterize your communications.

Also, the danger exisits that others may not be playing politics as ethically as you are. To protect yourself against backstabbing, self-aggrandizing, deceitful players, consider the following:

- Give other people the benefit of the doubt. While their tactics may be questionable, they may be acting out of desperation, the tactics may not be typical of their behavior, or they may not have realized their actions were offensive.
- Look for "dirty tricks" that are played repeatedly by the same person. Sometimes telling tricksters you know what they are up to is enough to stop their deception.
- Do not trust blindly. As diplomatically as possible, question the source of information or ask how the data was acquired.
- If you have been "taken," yield the advantage but do not let the exchange conclude without saying something, such as "Next time I'll expect you to make the concession I made today."

- As tempted as you might be to join in gossiping, avoid it at all costs. It wastes time, it harms reputation, and it causes others to look upon the gossipers with disfavor.
- If you find yourself the object of office rumors (perhaps being spread by someone with a malicious reason for putting you in a bad light) confront him or her directly. Ask to meet with the person you believe is spreading the rumors. You can either deny the rumors or admit to their truth if you choose to do so. You can take the wind out of the gossip sails by holding your head high and speaking the truth. In a short time, the gossiper will find other things to do and other topics to discuss.

Advantages of Being Political

If you are open-minded enough to consider the benefits to be derived from being political, then you can acknowledge that effective office politicians know how to strategize, how to maximize available resources, and how to apply psychological principles to everyday actions.

Further, if you are a good player in the political game, you have probably developed your persuasive skills and acquired vision regarding the future. In fact, the master strategist Winston Churchill once defined political skill as "the ability to foretell what is going to happen tomorrow, next week, next month, and next year." Looking ahead means spotting potential pitfalls before they cause damage. It also means making and preparing for a future you help to create.

Office politicians know how to get things done—often in the easiest way possible. While politicians do cut corners, they never do so at the risk of harming others or impeding progress toward the goal. Yes, they are ambitious, but think about how many things you enjoy today that are the result of an ambitious person's drive. Those who are "politic," according to the dictionary's first definition, "have practical wisdom." They are "prudent, shrewd, and diplomatic." Yes, political behavior can be applied to unscrupulous ends, but not by those who lead in an ethical fashion.

The practical wisdom politicians employ is probably most evident in their words. Having the right words and knowing when to use them can affect personal success, cooperative relationships and workplace harmony. Politicians, whether they are public servants or organizational servers, who fail to choose their words wisely often find themselves losing supporters. Witness the careers of the Arizona Governor who was impeached, the Vice President who misspelled *potato*, and the President who had trouble defining the word *is*.

If you are politic in your words and actions, your decisions can become turning points in the lives of others. Of course, the reverse is true as well. Many historians, for example, believe that Grover Cleveland achieved his Presidential victory and Catholic support because his Republican opponent unwisely used these alliterative words: "Rum, Romanism, and Rebellion."

> *"Every high-level political decision is risky."*
> **—Betty Lehan Harragan**

Harragan is correct, of course, in recognizing the riskiness of high-level political decisions. But even low-level political decisions are risky. They can backfire and cause embarrassment, they can even damage careers. When foraying into new office territory, getting to know a powerful figure better, or undertaking a project that will bring you visibility, for example, you are simultaneously taking some risks. You may lose your way in the new terrain, you may be rejected by the power figure, you may see the project fail and find yourself tainted in the process. Just remember, though, that if no (political) thing is ventured, no thing is gained.

Disadvantages of Being Political

- *Communication Breakdowns.* Every organization has serious power brokers. They are usually quite political by nature. If they operate with win/win intentions, you can gain a great deal by associating with them. Be forewarned, however, that your association may be viewed by jealous colleagues as an attempt on your part to infiltrate the upper echelons. You need courage to take this risk of association.

The less secure may bad-mouth you; they may assume your efforts are less than honorable. Additionally, your efforts to know some power brokers better may be misconstrued by the power brokers themselves. You must think long and hard about your approach. Think about the best way to communicate that you are more than a political wanna-be. You are a person who views politics and political associations as a means to an altruistic end.

- *Creation of a Climate of Fear.* If the playing of the political game has become an end in itself, if the game is more important than its purpose, or if the rules are changed or ignored (in short, if politics is practiced for selfish or arbitrary reasons), every-

©PhotoDisc, Inc.

one loses. The players lose because sooner or later they will encounter someone who plays the game of deceit better than they. The organization loses because the nonplayers are fearful of what their exclusion means, and the fear that develops ultimately erodes trust, collegiality, and other positive (nonmonetary) reasons why people enjoy their work.

- *Waste of Valuable Resources.* Politics can have a corrosive effect on people. Distrust can set in. Missions can be scoffed at. Interpersonal relationships can disintegrate into camps of "us" versus "them." These outcomes represent a waste of organizational resources. Few organizations can afford such waste. Besides human resources are not being optimized.

Tools, Tips and Techniques

You need not be regarded as only a "player" in the political game; you can often emerge the winner. The rules of this game, unfortunately, change rapidly and are not written down. To be political means to develop an awareness of who/what succeeds and who/what fails. As you do so, keep in mind that office politics should not be a source of sin, shame, or sugarcoating. You can take ethical, proud, and direct actions and, at the same time, serve your colleagues well. Let the following tools, tips, and techniques guide you.

- *Suggest a trial period, If you meet opposition to an idea you are proposing.* If you are as successful as you are confident, you can then ask to have the trial period extended.
- *Learn about the political climate in which you are working.* This means knowing, among other things, what actions have led to failure for others, knowing who is "in" and why, determining who is "out" and why, and learning what behaviors lead to promotion.
- *Volunteer to do the jobs no one else wants to do.* Pitching in occasionally shows your willingness to get the job done. However, do not make this your trademark; you do not want others to think they can take advantage of you.
- *Work hard to meet the needs of those in authority.* Make certain you fully understand management's requirements; then go out of your way to meet them. If in time you do not think you are getting the recognition or respect you deserve, make your own needs known.
- *Seize opportunities.* When you are not certain if a possibility is an opportunity, seek the advice of someone whose opinion you respect. Find ways to benefit from every experience, even the negative ones.
- *Learn continuously.* Whether you read avidly, take courses, or simply observe/analyze what is happening in the work environment, add to your knowledge on a daily basis.
- *Plan.* Know what your desired outcomes are before you take action.
- *Gain visibility in circles above the immediate one.* Curry favor or at least recognition from your supervisor's manager. Do not skip links in the chain of command; rather, try to make yourself known in the normal course of events.
- *Make comparisons.* Notice who is moving ahead. Compare yourself to the activities/personalities/background/words of those in whose steps you would like to follow.
- *Give credit.* You never know who may be in a position to hurt or harm you. Consequently, the best policy is to treat everyone with respect and dignity. Show your appreciation to everyone who has helped you. Do not steal credit that belongs to someone else.
- *Develop your communication skills.* Improve your ability to write, speak, read, respond quickly, and think critically.
- *Reinvent (or at least recalibrate) yourself from time to time.* Take stock at least once a year of your goals, your progress, and your aspirations. Look at your current patterns of operation, and determine where

improvement is needed. Think about the alliances you need to make and perhaps those you need to break.

- *Learn your supervisor's preferences.* The more you are in sync with your supervisor's style, wishes, and preferences, the better you can do your job. However do not be a rubber stamp. Rather, work the way your manager works. When necessary, suggest better ways of doing things.
- *Keep secrets—your own and others'.* Resist the temptation to tell all. Not only do you run the risk of being labeled a gossip, but if you share too much about yourself, your words can come back to haunt you. If you are revealing information told to you in confidence, you are bound to lose the trust and respect of those who originally confided in you.

> *"Knowledge of human nature is the beginning and end of political education."*
>
> **—Henry Adams**

RECAP OF KEY CONCEPTS

- Politics has been defined as "the art of the possible." Handled ethically and effectively, politics can make good things happen.
- *Politics* is a neutral word, one that can have either positive or negative connotations. Ideally, you are using office politics to bring about overall improvements, not just improvements in your own status.
- When you decide to improve your political savvy, you are making good use of the skills you already have (strategizing, forecasting, persuading, and relating on an interpersonal level) but you are also developing new ones.
- Communication breakdowns can occur when you concentrate only on getting ahead and not getting your work done. Further, your actions can instill fear or misunderstanding in others. Excessive politicking, especially politicking of the negative kind, can result in a waste of valuable resources.
- Advancing your understanding of human nature is the best way to educate yourself politically. Commit to being a continuous learner in the field of human nature.

8
Teambuilding

T eams come in many sizes and shapes and names. In addition to regular teams, you have QITs (Quality Improvement Teams), PITs (Process Improvement Teams), CATs (Continuous Action Teams), PAT (Process Action Teams), PIGs (Process Improvement Groups), CITs (Continuous Improvement Teams), ad hoc groups, and self-directed work teams. No matter what the name, though, all teams have some things in common, as discussed below.

The Role of a Team

Most importantly, teams are expected to get the jobs to which they have been assigned completed on time and within budget. In addition, they are expected to be disciplined, cooperative, and focused on a common goal. Teams are collections of like-minded individuals focused on a single goal. They meet regularly to accomplish that goal.

Teams enjoy a multiplicative power —the energy that is released from members' collective efforts, sometimes referred to as synergy. Teams, especially when they are successful with their early projects, are energized to tackle projects of increasing difficulty. However, if initial projects fail, teams members may be so discouraged that they hesitate to join other teams in the future. Prudent selection of projects is a critical first step in the success of a team.

Teams are expected to put forth their best to attain an organizational goal. If a team's work is not supporting the company's mission, the team should not be functioning. To engage in a pursuit that is not directly connected to an organization's purpose is to behave in a fraudulent manner. This awareness of mission can often serve as a determining factor when decisions have to be made.

Usually, a team project supports an organization's current mission. If that mission will undergo change in the near future, the team is wasting its time engaging in the project until circumstances determine the necessity of the project.

Whether your team's mission statement has been foisted on you or whether you have been able to create it, ensure that it:

- Is clearly articulated.
- Is supported by each team member.
- Reflects the expectations that have been made known to you.
- Specifies boundaries.
- Has been approved and funded.
- Parallels the larger organizational goals.
- Is realistic.

The Team Makeup

Research shows ideal teams to have seven or eight members. (Size, of course, is no guarantee of success or of failure.) Typically, teams operate under the guidance of a team leader who involves all members, is familiar with the talents of each member, knows how to manage conflict (not eliminate it), understands team dynamics, and periodically assesses the team's success. Team leaders are also dedicated to the team's mission and know how to inspire without pushing, obtain approval without fawning, and celebrate without gloating.

Obviously, you want committed, contributing, cooperative individuals who believe in the mission and are determined to fulfill it. Passion goes a long way toward making great things happen. You also want individuals who treat time and one another with respect. Ground rules help ensure respect. Just as a mission is the overarching frame of reference for a team's ultimate accomplishment, ground rules serve as the overarching frame of reference for the team's day-by-day operation. Work with your team to compose ten rules that engender respect for both time and other people.

Team Development Stages

Bruce Tuckman's model of team formation, which follows, reflects the stages of team development, but it does not reflect the slippage that may occasionally occur. Team buildling is not a linear progression. Only in the broadest, most general terms does a team move out of one stage and into the next. For example, having passed the initial Storming stage does not mean the end to all conflict and Norming is not a one-time occurrence. New norms may have to be considered throughout the Performing stage.

Nonetheless, the four-word rhyme that follows is a useful construct for advising team members of what is likely to occur as they act and interact with one another. Realize, though, that a team may occasionally take a step backward for the many steps it takes forward. There are generally four stages in the formation of teams.

Stage 1: Forming. When team members convene, they are typically uncertain about what to expect. As a result, they turn to the team leader for information, for introductions, for the establishment of guidelines, and so on. During this stage, the team leader can exert considerable influence on the team, its structure, and its ultimate success.

Because members at this stage are guarded, uncertain, and not willing to reveal much about themselves, the team leader has to establish an atmosphere of harmony and trust in order to optimize time and talent. Because the members have questions they are not willing to ask, the team leader must anticipate such questions and provide answers.

Stage 2: Storming. At this stage, the team needs to identify its mission and write goals; establish a code of conduct; determine the resources needed to get the job done; and assign roles based on each individual's interests, expertise, and strengths. During this stage of team building, members begin to open up. They are more willing to disagree about values, priorities, goals, or tasks; demand clarification of roles and challenge the leader and each other; and rebel against decisions that go against their individual grain. Frequent confrontations are to be expected if the team is to learn about its composite membership. Growth seldom occurs without the weathering of interpersonal storms.

The team leader lets eruptions occur but not get out of control. He or she is usually more democratic than autocratic in this stage, operating from a "sell" stance without relinquishing complete authority. The team leader's primary objective at this point is to establish harmony within the team by adopting a problem-solving attitude.

Stage 3: Norming. Commitment is the operative word for the third stage of team formation. The team now congeals into a genuine group. Team members begin to offer their talents and to recognize the importance of the task before them. Now the leader is consulting with members and willingly sharing the leadership role. Because commitment is growing, the criticality of the mission begins to override the importance of individuals' needs. In the norming stage, team members begin to find ways to accomplish their task more efficiently. They are willing to trade off, to share, and to experiment. Their enthusiasm is surging.

In optimizing this stage, the team leader and members alike need to open up, to dissent, and to make their needs known. Just as the only stupid question is the one you are afraid to ask, the only stupid decision is the one based on hidden agendas. Mutual trust has formed a foundation upon which cooperation and team spirit build. The team leader moves into the role of a facilitator who keeps the team headed in the right direction.[9]

> "What lies behind us and what lies before us are tiny matters, compared to what lies within us."
>
> **—Oliver Wendell Holmes**

Stage 4: Performing. The final stage of team building represents the idealized version of the process. The team leader does not need to control as he or she did at the beginning. Now the leader essentially joins the team as a member on equal footing. The leader knows the team has acquired the necessary power as an integrated unit, thereby relinquishing his or her power. Team members at this stage share; they display commitment to the common goal; they cooperate; they know what lies within them. Team members have learned how to give and take criticism, and they enjoy working with one another and working toward a shared purpose. They experience pride in what they can accomplish as a united whole.

Team building is simply the process of developing a cohesive group of individuals committed to working cooperatively and achieving high performance in pursuit of organizational aims. If you are the team leader or facilitator, you have a special responsibility to ensure that the team functions at optimal efficiency. Even as a regular team member, you can contribute to a positive working relationship among members of the group. If you are skilled at bringing harmony to group interactions, you are fortunate indeed. Optimizing team effort is a skill that can be used in any number of work and nonwork situations.

In the process of building a team, conflicts inevitably occur. However, conflict can be made to work for rather than against you. Conflict can actually lead to greater team commitment and cooperation. A cohesive group that has weathered the storms of conflict together invariably achieves greater success than the team that flounders and sinks in the seas of conflict.

> "What we must decide is perhaps how we are valuable, rather than how valuable we are."
>
> **—Edgar Friedenber**

The First Meeting

Initial team meetings are very important; they set the tone that is likely to remain throughout the course of the team's existence. They start the process of cohesion, of seeing just how valuable this group is as individuals and how they can be valuable in the accomplishment of a project.

In the Forming stage, members invariably have questions. The team leader addresses them and also answers unasked questions about mission, commitment of resources, sponsorship, and the elements that constitute both success and failure. While a team can provide its members with a great source of satisfaction, the team can also be a source of frustration. It takes wise leadership and willing membership to prevent the latter. The following is a list of questions team members often bring to the first meeting. They may not voice them, but they are thinking them. To be sure, teams deserve prompt and complete answers to these questions:

1. What are the goals?
2. Who provides the mission statement?
3. What are our limits?
4. Where will support come from? Who will be our sponsor?
5. Who will be team leader? How is he or she selected?
6. What are the deadlines we face?
7. What resources are available?
8. What data will we need to collect?
9. For how long will our team exist?
10. Who are our customers? What do they expect of us?
11. Will our team responsibilities conflict with our regular jobs?
12. What is the reward for success?
13. How will decisions be made?
14. How will our efforts be measured?
15. Will our intended success be replicated? If so, how and by whom?

Boundaries are set both internally and externally. The external ones have to be considered first. Someone in authority has approved the formation of your team. This individual or group of individuals also should have defined your mission, advised you of budgetary constraints, informed you of available resources, made you aware of the scope of your authority, clearly designated the team's responsibility, and designated milestone dates by which you must meet certain goals. If this information has not been made available to you, you must ask for clarification. Operating in the dark wastes everyone's time.

Once team members have assembled, you need to obtain agreement on the viability of the boundaries given to you. If certain members cannot conform to expectations, the group must decide what to do. For example, if a team lacks expertise for accomplishing the mission, the team can obtain training, invite a person with the necessary expertise to be part of the team, or invite an outsider to attend select meetings to offer his or her expertise.

After the first meeting, agendas virtually form themselves, but the first meeting is the most critical because it establishes the construct within which future meetings will take place. Questions are answered at that meeting, of course, but before that occurs, the team leader should spend time on the following:

- *The Social*
  A warm-up activity may be used to break the metaphoric ice. Everyone should introduce him- or herself—the team leader (if he or she has already been appointed), each member, and the sponsor. The leader should present the agenda.

- *The Statement*
  The mission statement should be explored at length and questions relevant to it answered in depth.

- *The Structure*
  Administrative issues are covered in this part of the meeting. Ground rules, for example, are established, roles defined, questions answered, expectations clarified, the sponsor's role explained, housekeeping matters attended to (meeting rooms, times, refreshments), and assignments distributed and dates confirmed for reporting the results of those assignments.

Team Barriers

Barriers can be found in the very nature of team members. If the team is composed of individuals vying for power and visibility, the team cannot reach collective success. In the ideal team, the objective takes precedence over individual priorities. Members must let go of their egos long enough to seek the synergy that is released when people are committed to collaborative interaction.

Autocratic behavior on the part of the team leader can also create barriers. Except in crisis situations, such behavior is not effective. Team members are independent. They seek fulfillment and satisfaction in their work. They want the pride associated with accomplishment. They are willing to give, but they also expect to recieve. They anticipate working on a team that functions well, knowing that when skills are blended and conflict is resolved, members get a return on their effort investment—they get back the satisfaction derived from attaining a goal.

The Nominal Group Technique is a useful tool for moving beyond the barriers born of division—when half the team wants one thing and the other half wants something else or when nearly everyone agrees on one approach but a few dissenters hold up progress. The technique begins with a list of options being considered; up to 20 is a good, manageable number. Each person is given four cards. He or she then makes four choices and writes one choice on each card. The top choice for each member is given the number 4, written on the card with that choice. The second-favorite choice is given a 3, the next favorite is given a 2, and the least favorite of the person's top four choices is given a 1. The votes are tallied, and the choice (from the original list of 20) garnering the highest score is the one the team goes with.

Just because the team decides to proceed in this fashion does not necessarily mean the opinion of the opposition should be ignored. If the one person objecting finally agrees to accept the consensus vote but still has reservations, note in the record the concerns of this person.

The Team Sponsor

Also called coaches, champions, advisors, and facilitators, team sponsors have far-reaching roles. Clearly, the more sophisticated the team members, the less dependence they will have on their sponsor. But even the most sophisticated teams occasionally have need for the clout a sponsor can wield. Having an advocate who can walk "mahogany row" without bumping into walls ensures a distinct advantage.

Your sponsor may be asked to share his or her expertise. This expertise may pertain to the content of your meetings; it may also pertain to context: group dynamics, meeting process, decision making, and so on. Sponsors, because of their experience and proximity to senior management, can also offer advice on the politics of having your proposals accepted.

You can call upon your sponsor for general advice, for political insight, and for training in a specific arena. You can also ask your sponsor to help troubleshoot a particularly thorny issue that is causing conflict for the team. The sponsor may coach individual members or the team as a whole, but use him or her as a liaison between the team and senior management. Have your sponsor help you prepare persuasive presentations, convince others your proposals should be accepted, aid in implementation, and (worst-case scenario) accept rejection.

The most suitable sponsor for one project may not be the most suitable for another. Much depends on the voids that exist in the team's makeup. Since those voids vary, the kind of sponsor varies too. A team with considerable knowledge of finance, for example, does not need a sponsor skilled in that area of expertise.

Generally, you want the sponsor to be someone from inside the organization who is familiar with the system, has some political authority, is a good teacher, helps you obtain resources, provides a comprehensive view of the big picture, helps you establish priorities, helps you avoid mistakes and diminish the impact if mistakes occur; and relates well to others. You also want a sponsor who is not so overburdened that he or she has little time to assist your team. In short, do not expect your sponsor to:

- Be available at the drop of a hat.
- Attend all your meetings.
- Fight all your battles (internal or external).
- Handle administrative matters.
- Take sides.
- Continuously praise.
- Ignore wrinkles that are spotted in the fabric of your teamwork.
- Sugarcoat or remain aloof.
- Take full responsibility for the team or control all aspects of team functioning.

In short, do not expect your sponsor to solve all your problems. To illustrate, if the team has never before managed a project or has not done data collection, your sponsor can help you discover best practices; however, you cannot expect him or her to supply all the answers or dictate the way things should be done.

While your sponsor has a general awareness of what is happening with your team day by day, he or she is not directly involved. Instead, your sponsor knows your deadlines and is around before they arrive to ensure they are met. Your sponsor is available to help you handle obstacles. He or she sits in when conflict is demoralizing the team and when the team needs training in a particular skill, but the sponsor does not hold team members' hands. The sponsor expects that, as a team, you are already standing. His or her job is to help you reach the finish line as victors.

- Above all else, teams are expected to complete the assignment they have been given—on time, within budget, and according to accepted organizational standards.
- An important factor contributing to a team's success is size. Research shows that ideal teams have seven or eight members.
- Well-built teams cooperate, they share communal successes and failures as if they were their own. Such teams have undergone the stages of team formation—Forming, Storming, Norming, and Performing.
- At the first meeting, team members bring fear, discomfort, and many questions. The leader's team-building skills undergo the first test at this time. The team's purpose is made clear to participants, and an agenda of planned discussion items is presented.
- Personality issues often present barriers. Egos, autocratic leaders, and different points of view—all of these can drag down a team's morale. One tool that helps resolve differences is the Nominal Group Technique; it allows team members to make their choices known more than once.

A team sponsor should be someone from inside the organization who serves as an advocate. This person should be someone who is familiar with the system, who has some political authority, who is a good teacher, who helps you obtain resources, who provides a comprehensive view of the big picture, who helps you establish priorities, and who helps you avoid mistakes.

9

Handling Conflict

AT THE CORE

This topic examines:

➤ **CAUSES OF WORKPLACE CONFLICT**

➤ **SIGNS OF POTENTIAL VIOLENCE**

➤ **THE K-I-N-D TECHNIQUE**

➤ **THE E-N-D RESULT**

➤ **THE AWE-FILL APPROACH**

➤ **DIVERSIONARY TACTICS**

➤ **THE QUESTION APPROACH**

et's face it. The world is not a perfect place and there are no perfect people inhabiting it. The best we can hope for is people's willingness to improve life's circumstances. If we are truly committed to the idea of reducing workplace conflict, there is much we can do to inspire such willingness in others.

When conflict is not resolved, when it is allowed to fester, it is often expressed in hostile, aggressive, and violent ways. But you can take precautionary steps to ward off such outcomes by using techniques such as the K-I-N-D Technique, the E-N-D Result, and the AWE-FILL Approach. They will help you help others, help yourself, and help your organization.

> *"Out of clutter, find simplicity. From discord, find harmony. In the middle of difficulty lies opportunity."*
>
> **—Albert Einstein**

While you may not see the connection between clutter and conflict at first, you will probably come to realize that clutter adds to stress and that stress leads to less harmonious relationships between people. Commit to simplifying the processes of your work, simplifying your filing systems, and simplifying your life by getting rid of unnecessary possessions.

Follow Einstein's advice and commit to converting discord to harmony. This topic explores numerous ways for you to do so. Basically such a conversion requires less sense of self and more sense of others in order to put anger behind you and look forward to greater cooperation. As you work through these difficulties, you will find opportunities to enrich your professional life as well as your personal life.

Causes of Workplace Conflict

Issues of customer satisfaction, productivity, and quality are important issues in the workplace. However, pursuing them is difficult when employees are fighting with one another. How many people, after all, can keep up a brave front while being betrayed by coworkers? How many are willing to put oars into troubled waters when the wind is being taken out of their sails? How can you fight fire with fire if you are sinking in a sea of conflict, insults, and innuendos?

> *"The infinite capacity of human beings to misunderstand one another makes our jobs and our lives far more difficult than they have to be."*
>
> **—Anonymous**

Metaphors aside, if you want to "reengineer" work processes, you need workplace engineers who can work together. If you are going to manage quality, you first have to manage yourself. If you intend to thrive on economic/technological chaos, you first need to control the interpersonal chaos in the office.

At times, of course, the chaos may seem beyond your control. In these uncertain times involving the work world, emotions are close to the surface and tensions run rampant. In fact, definitions regarding the tension surrounding possible job loss appear frequently and humorously: "Optimists bring their lunch to work. Pessimists leave the car running." Humor does help. So does reminding yourself that you always have choices. You can choose to understand or misunderstand, help or prevent, cooperate or antagonize, remain stagnant or move forward.

Bringing conflict into the open has its advantages. Talking about conflict often helps to clear the air, and thinking about the possibility of conflict often helps to avoid it. The following exercise can help you convert provocative statements into less offensive remarks before you actually utter them. Try changing these abrasive remarks into less destructive statements, or think of a humorous rejoinder that could be applied if and when such abrasive statements are made.

a. "That's the dumbest thing I ever heard."
b. "If we had some people in this office who knew what they were doing, we could get more done."
c. "If our manager would just lead, we might be able to accomplish the mission."
d. "I don't have time for all this 'exploration.' Let's just choose a course of action and move forward."
e. "Some people around here contribute nothing. If we're not all going to pull our own weight, then I'm out of here."

Of course, it is not just the threat of unemployment that causes tempers to flare and harsh words to be uttered. It is a wide range of stimuli, both inside and outside the workplace. Taken to an extreme, workplace anger can lead to homicidal results. In fact, every week in the United States, 20 people are killed in the workplace. In addition, the Bureau of Labor Statistics reports that another 18,000 are assaulted each week while at work or on duty.

Signs of Potential Violence

Conflict in the workplace, like many other issues, is hard to define and difficult to measure. What one person regards as conflict, another person may simply accept as curmudgeonly behavior. These issues are seldom black or white. Instead, they usually appear as multiple shades of gray. At the extreme, though, conflict means unacceptable violence, violence that, according to experts, can be minimized through prehiring checks and alert coworkers.[10]

What exactly should alert coworkers look for? What are the behaviors that, in the aggregate, indicate the potential for violence? Among them are the following:

- Repeated and excessive use of alcohol
- History of aggressive behavior
- Pronounced lack of self-confidence/self-esteem
- Unexplained increase in absenteeism
- Noticeable decrease in attention to appearance and hygiene
- Depression and withdrawal
- Explosive outbursts of anger or rage without provocation
- Repeated comments that may indicate suicidal tendencies
- Undiagnosed or undetected mental illness
- Noticeably unstable emotional responses
- Paranoid behavior
- Preoccupation with previous incidents of violence
- Increased mood swings
- Resistance and overreaction to changes in procedures
- Increase of unsolicited comments about firearms and other dangerous weapons
- Repeated violations of company policies
- Fascination with violent and/or sexually explicit movies or publications
- Escalation of domestic problems[11]

"God did not create junk. He only created people with behavior problems."

—*Anonymous*

Among the choices you can make to reduce conflict is the commitment to understand behavior better—your own and others'. There are numerous articles, web sites, and books on the subject. Decide at what end of the continuum the behavior problem lies. Is the conflict-causing action a mere irritant? Handle it yourself. (You will find several tools for doing so in the following section.) Does it have the potential for tragic results? Follow company policy for dealing with such actions, and/or refer the matter to someone in authority.

The K-I-N-D Technique

With conflicts that appear at the lower or middle point on the continuum, you can apply strategies such as the K-I-N-D Technique. The letters stand for:

K	=	Kind
I	=	Informed
N	=	New
D	=	Definite

The technique involves your requesting a meeting with the difficult person, whether he or she is having a conflict with you or with others. Start off with kind words, words that encourage cooperation, words that evince your determination to make the conflict situation better. Next, demonstrate that you have taken the time to learn more about the person, what is important to him or her, what he or she prefers in terms of work. Show by your words that you have taken the time to become informed about the individual.

The third step requires you to do something novel, something you have not tried before. Put your creativity to work, and discover a plan to which you can both subscribe (for example, keeping a journal regarding the problem and possible solutions).

Finally, do not permit the exchange to conclude until you have made a definite overture to ensure future success. What can you promise the other person you will do differently? What are you asking him or her to do differently? Set a time to meet again and review your individual attempts to achieve collective improvement.

The E-N-D Result

Seek to understand the other person before automatically ascribing negative intentions to his or her words or behavior. Keep uppermost in your mind the reason why you are in the workplace to begin with—not to argue with a coworker, but to accomplish a particular objective, mission, or goal. Because the departmental or organizational mission overrides your particular concern, you must keep the end result in mind. To do that, you will find this acronymic method helpful.

E = Enlist the person's help. Point out that the stress you two are generating is doing neither one of you any good. Nor is it having a positive effect on others in the workplace.

N = Negotiate. Explain exactly what bothers you and why. Patiently listen as the other person does the same. Tell what you are willing to do differently. Ask the other person to do the same.

D = Determine specific steps each of you can and will take next.

The Awe-Fill Approach

Becoming familiar with a conflict-reducing technique—so familiar that its use becomes second nature—will enable you to think easily and well in the face of pressure. When you are caught off guard, your mind may go blank. However, having a familiar, dependable technique to use allows you to fill in the blanks.

The letter A stands for *Assert*. Make a strong statement when a dispute arises. Then apply the W: *Withdraw*. Back off a bit. Lessen the severity of the statement you have just made. Next, *Encourage* an exchange of ideas. Be ready to *Fill* the conversation with details. The following dialogue between supervisor and subordinate illustrates the technique. In this case, the employee is using AWE-FILL with her manager.

Employee (Assert):	I don't appreciate being criticized in front of others.
Supervisor:	You're overreacting, Megan. Is there something else going on in your life that's affecting you?
Employee (Withdraw):	Nothing's bothering me except your way of doing public appraisals of my performance. However this is a problem I'm sure we can resolve.
Supervisor:	Consider it resolved.
Employee (Encourage):	I'd like to set up an appointment to talk about it.
Supervisor:	Neither of us has time for something that trivial.
Employee (Fill):	Actually, it's not the first time it's happened; it's happened with others as well. I don't want to make this more of an issue than it needs to be, but the fact remains that we need to talk about this.

Diversionary Tactics

When you find someone starting to show anger or distress, your first reaction may be to tell them to calm down. This is one of the worse things you can say because it implies that the other person has lost control of his or her composure. Try a diversionary tactic rather than telling the person to calm down.

For example, if someone is angry and shouting at you regarding a lost invoice, do not immediately make apologies. Instead, try asking a question: "Do you know, Mr. Johnson, how often we lose invoices on an annual basis?" The person will have to stop his tirade to answer your question. Then you can proceed to explain that losing as invoice is a rare occurrence but one you will work hard at to prevent happening again.

The Question Approach

According to Peter Drucker, often regarded as the Father of Modern Management Science, leaders know how to ask questions, the right questions. You should keep certain questions in your mental reserves so you can pull them out when conflict begins to erupt.

Look at the dialogue below. Ling's use of questions helps to defuse the potential conflict rather than escalate it.

Arlene: I don't like the way you handled that customer complaint.

Ling: What exactly didn't you like?

Arlene: You didn't tell her about the options available in the new checking account.

Ling: Tell me something, Arlene. Do you think I did that deliberately?

Arlene: No, not really.

Ling: You're right. It was an oversight on my part. Now I can either call her about those options or mail her the brochure that describes them.

If Ling had not used questions, the dialogue might have sounded like this:

Ling: I don't like the way you handled that customer complaint.

Ling: And I don't like your attitude!

Arlene: The only thing worse than *your* attitude is your incompetence when it comes to customers.

Ling: You should talk! What about your incompetence when it comes to errors on requisitions.

RECAP OF KEY CONCEPTS

- ◆ Daily news reports often make it seem that the world is a powder keg, ready to explode. Such stress makes people tense, even before they reach the workplace. Add personal problems to this tension and you have the potential for conflict every day. However, you can choose to defuse, rather than contribute to workplace friction.

- ◆ Be alert to signs of violence. Do not try to handle extreme cases yourself: You are not trained to do so. For everyday conflicts, though, there are several techniques you can employ.

- ◆ For conflict that falls at the lower or middle point on the continuum, consider conflict-reduction strategies such as the K-I-N-D Technique. Begin with a kind word. Then show you have taken the time to acquire information about the individual. Next, try a new overture to resolving the conflict. End with a definite suggestion for follow-through.

- ◆ The E-N-D Result asks you to enlist the other person's help in fashioning a win/win outcome. From that point, you negotiate the terms that will help each of you achieve the outcome. Finally, you determine specific actions to be taken next.

- ◆ When you use the AWE-Fill Approach, you make an assertion from which you then withdraw. Next, you encourage an exchange with the other person whose behavior is causing the conflict. Then be ready to fill in blanks in the dialogue with specific details.

- ◆ Diversionary tactics work best when you need to divert the flow of emotional traffic. Getting the other person's mind off his or her anger allows time for a respite and prevents a volatile situation from escalating.

- ◆ Use questions to lead an interpersonal exchange away from negativity and toward positive ends.

Case Studies

Case Study #1 The Supervisor Who Fails to Reprimand

Your supervisor is a thoroughly likeable person. She is kind, thoughtful, efficient, and absolutely committed to giving credit where credit is due. The problem is this: she is hesitant to criticize or reprimand. The situation has deteriorated to the point where some employees are actually taking advantage of her nonauthoritative style. You have decided to meet with her in order to improve the situation.

Outline the points you would make.

_____

_____

_____

_____

Case Study #2 Senior Workers Versus Entry-Level Workers

You have been in your position for 29 years and are proud of the contributions you have made over the years. You would like to continue sharing your expertise by helping recently hired employees. However, there is a group of "nexters" (people born after the year 1980) whose outlooks and attitudes differ considerably from your own. For example, not believing they are entry-level workers, they expect to be accorded the privileges that come with having "paid your dues."

List at least five steps you (and possibly others) can take to achieve greater workplace harmony.

_____

_____

_____

_____

_____

_____

Case Study #3 The Need for a Leadership Development Program

You have learned that in some organizations, potential leaders are identified early and given extra training/assignments/introductions that will help them fast-track their careers. Your organization, however, does not have such a leadership-development program.

Prepare a persuasive argument that would convince senior management of the value of developing such a program.

_____

_____

_____

_____

_____

_____

Endnotes

Topic 1 – People Skills

1. Marlene Caroselli, *Richuals: 52 Ways to Enrich the Workplace*, CPD Press, Rochester, New York, 1999.
2. Marilyn Elias, "Bossier preschool kids are healthier," *USA Today*, March 8, 2000, p. 6D.
3. "Stress, Death and the Need for Control," *Executive S.O.S.*, a publication of Take Charge Consultants, Inc., Vol. 7, No. 2, Fall 1996, p. 3.
4. "Stress, Death and the Need for Control," *Executive S.O.S.*, a publication of Take Charge Consultants, Inc., Vol. 7, No. 2, Fall 1996, p. 3.

Topic 5 – Empowering Yourself

5. Ibid.

Topic 6 – Coaching and Mentoring Others

6. Lee Smith, "The Executive's new Coach," *Fortune*, 128:16, December 27, 1993, p.126.
7. Reid, Barbara Addison, "Mentorships Ensure Equal Opportunity," *Personnel Journal*, November 1994, pp. 122-123.
8. Kenneth Reynold, "The Importance of Mentoring," *CFO*, February 1995, p.76.

Topic 8 – Teambuilding

9. Debra Housel, *Team Dynamics*, (Cincinnati: South-Western Educational and Professional Publishing, 2002), p. 27.)
10. Marilyn Elias, "Laid-off workers more likely to flare," *USA Today*, August 16, 1994, p. D1.

Topic 9 – Handling Conflict

11. S. Pantry, *Dealing with Aggression and Violence in Your Workplace*. London: Library Association Publishing, 1996.

Online Resources

1. People Skills
http://www.skillwithpeople.com
http://members.aol.com/Relationshop

2. Persuading Others
www.pertinent.com/pertinfo/business/persuasion
The various complexities that can arise whenever two or more people interact are explored at this site, which provides tips, tools, and techniques for dealing with difficult situations.
www.influenceatwork.com
Better relationships is the focus of this web site which offers contemporary views of relationship-building.

3. Thinking on Your Feet
www.bebeyond.com
This site examines the all-important ability to reply both intelligently and quickly to unanticipated prompts and provides visitors with a wide range of tools for developing that ability.

4. Leading Others
www.keirsey.com
The advantages of this site are its broad overview of the topic of leadership and its more specific recommendations for enhancing one's leadership potential.
www.ccl.org
The Center for Creative Leadership is known for its research into management areas, especially the area of leadership. Here you'll find empirical data as well as practical applications of the data.

5. Empowering Yourself
http://www.universal-empowerment.com
A global perspective on empowerment can be found at this site, which also suggests ways to take the examples and make them appropriate for individual and organizational use.
www.lightseed.com
An inspirational, uplifting message can be found at this web site, which is designed to help individuals overcome barriers on both personal and professional levels.

6. Coaching and Mentoring Others

http://www.mentoring-programs.com

To obtain benchmarking information about mentoring programs already in existence, visit this site and learn how to make such programs work in your own work situation.

http://lists.webvalence.com

Many organizations have solid coaching/mentoring policies already in place. You can obtain lessons learned to reduce your own learning curve in these areas.

7. Acquiring Political Savvy

www.mapnp.org

To learn more about using politics and power wisely and well, visit this site. It encourages accomplishment via ethical practices.

http://www.fastcompany.com/online/14/politics.html

The latest views on politic savvy can be found here. The information is written in a lively, upbeat style that is current and "savvy."

8. Teambuilding

http://www.teambuildinginc.com

You'll discover some new slants on an old topic at this site. Hackneyed truisms are avoided. Instead, the site visitor will learn about the pitfalls and successes inherent in the teambuilding journey.

9. Handling Conflict

http://www.colorado.edu/conflict

This site offers valuable insights on the topic of interpersonal conflict from a more academic, research-oriented perspective. If you are interested in learning what research studies have shown, this site has what you need.

http://www.acresolution.org

No matter what conflicts you and others are experiencing at work, someone else has already experienced them. At this site you learn about successful ways to cope with such conflicts.

Post-Assessment Activity

Directions: Read each of the following statements carefully. Circle T if the statement is true and F if the statement is false.

1. T F Psychology is but a small part of good workplace relationships.

2. T F Listening well means listening to both what is said and what is not said.

3. T F You should ask the person with whom you are talking if he or she wants your feedback.

4. T F List reduction refers to minimizing the causes of a given effect.

5. T F The best problem solvers are more creative than analytical.

6. T F You can use questions as an ethical guide to your behavior.

7. T F Leadership and the ability to communicate well are closely related.

8. T F The ability to think well on your feet can be acquired.

9. T F Quotations can be used for both skill-building and practice and also as tools in real-life situations.

10. T F Leadership means effecting positive change.

11. T F You should avoid attempting to acquire power.

12. T F Leaders build alliances.

13. T F Empowerment is a one-way street.

14. T F The Five IN model refers to better communication.

15. T F Coaching and mentoring are two completely different roles.

16. T F If you have a mentor, you should also be a mentee.

17. T F Only poorly managed workplaces engage in politics.

18. T F Being political can help your career.

19. T F You should suggest a trial period if you think your proposal will not be accepted.

20. T F The team purpose should parallel the organizational mission.

21. T F Conflict in newly formed teams is an expected stage of development.

22. T F Team members will have few questions at the first meeting.

23. T F There are detectable signs of potentially violent behavior.

24. T F Saying "Calm down" is an effective means of reducing tension.

25. T F As an effective leader, you can handle every kind of conflict yourself.

Notes